Smart Hiring

2nd Edition

The Complete Guide to
Finding and Hiring the
Best Employees

Robert W. Wendover

Sourcebooks, Inc.
Naperville, IL

7-31-98

Editorial: Todd Stocke
Cover Design: Scott Theisen
Interior Design and Production: Scott Theisen, Sourcebooks, Inc.

This publication is designed to provide accurate and authoritative information in regard to the subject matter covered. It is sold with the understanding that the publisher is not engaged in rendering legal, accounting, or other professional service. If legal advice or other expert assistance is required, the services of a competent professional person should be sought.

From a Declaration of Principles Jointly Adopted by a Committee of the American Bar Association and a Committee of Publishers and Associations

Wendover, Robert W.
    Smart hiring : the complete guide to finding and hiring the best employees / Robert W. Wendover.—2nd ed.
        p. cm.
    Includes index.
    ISBN 1-57071-213-1 (alk. paper)
    1. Employee Selection—United States. I. Title.
HF5549.5.S38W467   1998
658.3'112—dc21

97-51870
CIP

Printed and bound in the United States of America.

Paperback — 10 9 8 7 6 5 4 3 2 1

Contents

Introduction

"I can't believe this!" said Jack. "Do you mean to say that after three weeks of advertising in the newspaper and hanging that huge sign in the window, we only have 12 applications?"

"That's what's happened," said Kate. "I told everyone I know to refer the best people they know and we got no response."

"Unbelievable!" said Jack.

"What makes matters worse," replied Kate, "is that half of the people who applied can't pass the math test. We either train them or look for other applicants."

"I don't understand," sighed Jack. "This time last year, we were turning people away."

It is official. The recruiting race has begun! Where we could once open the door and receive an abundance of applications, it is now necessary to search for applicants in most every industry. This is especially hard on the high turnover areas such as retail and fast-food. But our concerns are not just limited to locating applicants.

With cutbacks and an emphasis toward leaner organizations, every employee plays a more critical role. Poorly recruited staff means larger problems down the road. The traditional attitude about hiring has been, "When I need someone, I put an ad in the paper and hire, just like that," or "We need a warm body right now. If it doesn't work out, we can always get rid of him later."

But, hiring is just not what it used to be. Potential applicants have to be sold on the idea of working for a firm and then, once they have applied, they have to be screened carefully to insure a productive hire.

Adding to this is the tremendous cost of turnover. Replacing employees can run into the thousands, even for lower level positions. When the bottom line impact is factored into these equations, the overall expense can be devastating.

To stay on top of these challenges, old habits have to be changed. Those who are used to waiting for candidates to walk in the door have to go outside and drum up interest. Those who are accustomed to hiring teenagers will have to explore alternative sources of labor. And those who are used to hiring qualified applicants may find themselves spending more time on training.

Many times, little attention is paid to the hiring process with so many other tasks to be considered. But this haste can produce endless headaches. Someone hired in a rush to work in customer service may alienate a number of patrons before it's discovered she doesn't get along well with people. A new line manager may slow production because he was hired for a job over his head.

A host of new legal considerations have evolved making employees harder to hire and more difficult to fire. The Americans with Disabilities Act coupled with evolving civil rights and labor relations legislation can make hiring appear to be a legalistic maze. But the most successful employers find and maintain the balance between government mandates and crafting a fair, but demanding, selection process.

In addition to the legal and practical aspects, other factors can influence the hiring process.

Few plans are generally made to predict hiring's patterns and expansion. But many times, the needed labor pools do not exist when openings occur.

Many changes are taking place in the labor force. Traditional pools such as teenagers and college students, are decreasing in size.

Meanwhile the number of senior workers (those 55 and over) has increased dramatically. "Help wanted" signs have appeared in the windows of businesses that traditionally had more than enough applicants.

While the labor force will decrease in size, prospective employees must still be chosen carefully. Better personnel planning is needed to anticipate business demands.

Part-time employment has become a growing issue. Seniors are not often willing to work full-time. Women comprise more than half the work force. Immigration is altering the face of many labor pools. There is also an increased emphasis on leisure activities instead of long hours. Now, more than ever, employers must make the work environment both stimulating and satisfying.

Finally, decisions on disabilities, psychological screening, drug and AIDS testing, along with new interpretations of the anti-discrimination laws, have all affected the procedures for acquiring new employees.

Why This Book? To Save You Time and Money!

Smart Hiring has been written to provide a quick, easy-to-read handbook to assist any business in hiring effectively and legally. It is designed as a tool that can be referred to daily as hiring occurs.

- Use the principles in this book to pick the best applicant for the job.
- Understand the employment laws outlined here to avoid the common mistakes made when hiring.
- Place this book in the hands of your managers so they too will hire the right person for the right job.

Smart Hiring is specifically designed for the manager who has little or no experience in dealing with employee selection and its issues. Each chapter begins with an outline of what the reader will learn and concludes with a checklist of important guidelines. The text is outlined for easy reading and location of necessary principles along with sample forms and illustrations.

To get the most from this book, read it completely. Then place it in an easy-to-reach location for future reference. Treat this as a handbook. Use it the same way you would the Yellow Pages, as a daily resource for hiring effectively.

Hiring the Best Employees

"If each of us hires people who are smaller than we are, we shall become a company of dwarfs, but if each one of us hires people who are bigger than we are, Ogilvy & Mather shall become a company of giants."

—David Ogilvy, Chairman Emeritus, Ogilvy & Mather

Here's What You'll Learn

I. The Hiring Survival Checklist
II. Alternatives to Recruiting

How well do you perform the task of hiring? What characteristics make one candidate more attractive than the others? Do you hire giants or dwarfs?

The job you have is all consuming. You work day and night making sure that every detail is attended to. If a new employee is needed, your urge might be to hire the first reasonable person who walks through the door. You might call around to friends, acquaintances, and colleagues to see if they know someone reliable. But it's not that simple.

The Changing Work Force

A tremendous change is taking place in our nation's work force. According to the 1988 study *Work Force 2000*, four key trends will shape the last years of the twentieth century:

1. The U.S. economy should grow at a healthy pace boosted by a rebound in U.S. exports, renewed productivity growth and a strong economy.
2. Despite it's international comeback, U.S. manufacturing will be a much smaller share of the economy. Service industries will create virtually all of the new jobs and most of the new wealth.
3. The work force will grow slowly, becoming older, more female, and more disadvantaged.
4. The new service industry jobs will require significantly higher skill levels than the jobs of today. Few new jobs will be created for those who cannot read, follow directions and use mathematics. Ironically, the demographic trends in the work force coupled with the higher skill requirements of the economy will lead to both higher and lower unemployment, more joblessness for the lower skilled and less for the higher skilled.

Regardless of the size of your organization, these changes will have an impact on you. In hiring lower skilled workers for instance, you will discover an increasing need to provide training in basic skills. In higher skilled jobs, the competitions will be keener for qualified applicants. These applicants will come from more diverse backgrounds and experiences. There will be language barriers and many more will be female. Your organization's ability to adapt to these changes and use them to their advantage will determine your ability to compete successfully in the world economy. Hiring competent workers is no longer a option. It is a requirement for successful business. It requires anticipation of local markets in your community, long term planning of labor force movement, education, cultural balance and work ethic. How much do you know about these factors within your present labor force?

Cultural Diversity

In addition to numbers, the attitudes and culturalization of new work force entrants are becoming significantly different. The Hudson Institute has estimated that between now and the year 2000 the total number of native white males entrants to the work force will represent only 15 percent. Women will account for 67 percent and non-white and immigrant men will account for 20 percent. These figures have impacts on language work ethic and social barriers with which you, the employer, will have to deal. Work force entrants born after 1964 have known relative affluence and have not experienced the turmoil of previous generations. These attitudes combined with an abundance of jobs and a shortage of workers, will enable them to become more choosy about the positions they take regardless of being a higher or lower skilled position. Job security that so obsessed earlier generations now seems to mean little to these younger entrants.

With the shortage of labor, the expected abundance of applicants will not appear. This may further your urge to hire any warm body. But with the expense of turnover cutting into profits, staff selection without proper care is not an option. According to the Saratoga Institute, the average cost of hiring a first level supervisor was $7488 in 1990. For non-exempt employees, it was $652. How much does it cost you?

You may have hired employees before. Some worked out. Some did not. How can you do a better job of selecting peak performers?

I. The Hiring Survival Checklist

Before offering advice, it is important to understand your present position. What are your typical hiring practices?

Answer the questions below. There is no grading or rating scale attached, just an inventory of the process that should be practiced.

1. Do you hire "tens"?

According to management consultant I. Martin Jacknis, there is a tendency among supervisors to hire individuals who will not challenge their authority or influence. In other words, the "tens" (superior supervisors) will hire "nines." The nines will hire "eights" and the eights will hire "sevens." As David Ogilvy observes at the beginning of this chapter, continuing this practice makes the company an organization of dwarfs.

Encourage managers to look for the best person for the job regardless of the potential threat. It is commonly held that no one moves up until they have found someone to fill their present position. Finding an expert to do your job puts a feather in your cap.

2. Have you defined the kind of person that makes a good employee in your organization?

Whether you're a company of three or three hundred, a culture will exist. How do the other employees act? How hard do they work? How well do they get along? Is this a serious atmosphere? Does it lighten up? Is it downright fun?

What motivates these people? Do they share the company dream? How do you know? How did you select these people? What qualifications did these individuals have when they entered the company? Are there definite skills or experiences that all your employees have that are necessary for the manufacture or marketing of the product? Are "people skills" essential for the marketing of the product?

All of the above, in addition to other considerations specific to your situation will assist you in determining with consistency who might "fit-in." After all, performing the task is just part of the job. The manner in which new employees communicate with others is also critical.

3. Do you communicate your hiring goals to the rest of the company?

If the remainder of the organization is aware of the company's hiring needs, other employees will recruit suitable candidates. Informing employees of hiring policy creates and enforces an impression that everyone is involved in the process. This might be accomplished through a quick, two page newsletter from the president that examines the issue of "Where we are and where we're going." Something chatty and inspirational is usually effective.

4. Can you explain the hiring procedures that are used when hiring new employees?

Consistency is vital to the employee selection effort. As the organization grows and the occasional crisis takes place, there is a temptation to bend the rules to get a vacancy filled. These practices may have dire consequences in several ways: discrimination-related litigation, bad public relations both inside and outside the company, unacceptable turnover and declining employee morale. If the company is perceived as one that hires only people with an "inside track," other excellent candidates may not apply. These impressions are easily created through one or two questionable actions. In a small community, for example, rumors travel quickly if something is perceived to be wrong. Correcting impressions could take years.

5. When was the last time you examined the hiring procedures the company follows? Have the recommendations that resulted from that examination been implemented?

Who has time for something like this, right? But a cursory review of the procedures now in place may reveal some "interesting" items.

If you suspect some practice now in place might be improper, check your facts. Can someone really ask "that" question? Can we really say "this" in the job announcement?

Examine the entire process. What is being written in the classified ads? Does the standard application contain improper questions? Is the recordkeeping being maintained to satisfy government requirements? (See Appendix B for a complete list of federal requirements.)

The Digi-Lectronics Circuit

A monthly update of what's happening
Volume 34

New Distribution Jobs

Supervisor

Due to the increase in sales over the past six months, we will be hiring an additional distribution supervisor. This person should have a minimum of one year's experience in shipping (non-supervisory), knowledge of accounts receiveable and payable, and a demonstrated high energy work ethic.

This is a second shift position and will pay an 8% differential. Interested employees should contact Alex Raski's office ASAP. Referrals encouraged.

Shift Work

In addition to the supervisor's position, we are also seeking to fill a second shift of warehouse workers. These positions provide excellent opportunities for training and advancement to supervisory jobs. Those interested should apply to Rosemary Crena in shipping. Referrals encouraged.

Parking Lot Details

As petty as this sounds, we must insist that you park on the south side of the building for the rest of the time we are under construction. We know your cars are hot in the afternoon, but haphazard parking has cost the company a number of dollars.

Take Me Out to the Ballgame

We have purchased a block of tickets for the Reds & Mets game on June 30. If you qualify for two tickets from the incentive program, pick them up at Jean Simmon's desk by June 20. Those not redeemed by that time will be raffled off.

New Manuals Are In!

Those of you who requested personal copies of the circuit design for APA-36 can pick them up from Hank Ever's office any time. Digi-Lectronics will split the cost with you and your share is $12.50 along

continued on the next page

Sample newsletter page

Consider the decision making process. How was the last employee hired? Sit in on candidates' interviews to get a feel for what is occurring. What other details can you examine in your organization? One simple slip can be costly. "That's an interesting accent," observed one interviewer. "Where did you grow up?" Innocent question? Yes. Job related? No. Discriminatory? It could be viewed that way.

6. When was the last time you updated yourself on employee selection law and hiring technologies?

In this litigious society, the laws concerning employment change daily. It is not enough to rely on your attorney and accountant to warn you about potential liabilities. A solid working knowledge of these regulations is important, especially if you are responsible for most or all of the organization's hiring. (A thorough explanation of employment selection regulations is provided in Chapter Two).

The technology surrounding employee selection has grown more exacting. These strategies provide an employer with additional "sure-fire" means for selecting the best applicant. Many of the traditional strategies and questions have been replaced with more accurate procedures. Even pre-employment testing is making a comeback. (See Chapter Ten.)

7. How much does it cost for you to hire someone?

If you have not done so, calculate the cost of hiring for the various levels of employees within your organization. Are there ways to reduce these expenses by using different strategies or sources of applicants. For example, are you advertising every position in the newspaper when a number of these positions could be filled if you pressed your colleagues for additional referrals?

8. How much does it cost when an employee needs to be replaced?

This figure should include the cost of replacement, the additional training and staff commitment, and

> **Memorandum**
>
> To: Alex Raski, Vice President
>
> From: John Tutor, Customer Service Manager
>
> These are the estimated costs for replacing a receptionist as we did last week. It's obvious that this could get to be an expensive process.
>
> | | |
> |---|---|
> | Exit interview with manager @ $15/hr. | $15 |
> | Administrative paperwork @ $12/hr. | $12 |
> | Last day of work (exit interview, clean out desk, party, etc.) 8 hours @ $10/hr (incl. benefits) | $80 |
> | New hire selection costs (this has been our average) | $482 |
> | Training time (unproductive for 16 hours @ $10/hr.) | $160 |
> | Total | $749 |
>
> Note: This does not include unemployment compensation if necessary.

The cost of turnover

the lost work on the job. Seeing these expenses proves to be an effective motivator for re-examining your recruiting and training process.

9. *Do you regularly define the descriptions of vacant positions?*

The average company, large or small, does not have a complete set of job descriptions covering all positions. However, these documents are important. In addition to providing focus for the job, they may also serve as protection against litigation. A fired employee, for example, may sue for wrongful discharge. If the company is unable to produce even the most basic job description, it will be difficult to prove that the individual was released for not performing adequately on the job.

Finally, these descriptions serve as a road map for new employees. Supervisors can also benefit by familiarizing themselves with the "official" job descriptions of all those within their purview.

10. *Are you considering the versatility of the candidates?*

The average employee wears multiple hats. Will the person you hire be able to handle more than just the original responsibility? Are the skills of the final candidate too narrow to allow such a broadening?

It is not unreasonable to assume you will be able to find individuals with a myriad of talents. It just takes longer to find them. That's the reason for planning.

11. *Are you selling the advantages of working for your company?*

In a job shortage, everyone applies and you have no difficulty finding suitable applicants. But will the best ones stay when things get better?

Applicants need a "sales pitch" just as much as they need to make a good impression. Individuals on both sides should be on their best behavior. Explain how working in your company can benefit them. Discuss opportunities they might not have in other organizations. Explain the downside to make sure they understand the risks involved. If all of this is discussed during the hiring process, their understanding and commitment to the company will become apparent during crises and hard times.

One caveat here is to make sure you're selling the right person. Don't get so caught up in the "wonderfulness" of your company that you lose track of whether the candidate is suited for the job. Also be careful not to imply that the opening is a "permanent" or "career" position.

12. Have you analyzed the sources of your applicants?

Are some more fruitful than others? Could some means of recruiting be eliminated and others increased in order to improve effectiveness? Are there some sources from which you do not want applicants? It is always a good idea to start from the inside with referrals and proceed outward as the need warrants.

13. Do the right people do the hiring?

As organizations grow, the owners and executives sometimes retain crucial day-to-day duties that are best delegated. Too many times the founder hangs on to the responsibility for all hiring, even though s/he may not be in touch with the actual needs of a particular function. It is best to relinquish the responsibility to someone more directly related to the vacant position, like an immediate supervisor, provided that person is skilled in hiring.

Memorandum

To: All department managers

From: Alex Raski, Vice President

RE: Some thoughts on marketing the company to applicants

As we add a number of people to our organization over the next six months, I believe it is important to put our best foot forward. In regard to this, I have listed a few facts below to assist you in "selling" the applicants we want on coming to work for us.

Let's continue to build a great team!

We are the "fastest growing" electronics firm in the region according to *Daytona Business Journal* (April 6 issue)

Our sales have increased a minimum of 30% every year for the past five.

Our turnover rate among professionals is currently 4.5% (the lowest in the area for electronics firms according to our research.)

With the current Titan package being approved by Congress, we estimate that the contract alone will be responsible for 3 million dollars in income next fiscal year.

Our assembly technicians rated supervisory personnel 4.7 on a scale of 5.0 for attention to concerns.

We will be debuting a new product on the market in the next three months which should significantly change production schedules of printed circuit boards.

Our rejection rate on circuit assemblies is presently .6%, far below industry averages.

Just thought you'd like to know!

Marketing the company to applicants

Recruiting Evaluation

Position_____ Closing Date_____ Total # of applicants_____

Targeted applicant groups: _____

	Expense	Resulting Applicants	Comments
In-House Posting:	_____	_____	_____
Employee Ref:	_____	_____	_____
Classified Ads:	_____	_____	_____
Agency:	_____	_____	_____
Job Service:	_____	_____	_____
Other #1:	_____	_____	_____
Other #2:	_____	_____	_____
Recommendations:			_____

A president in one company of 250 employees insisted on reviewing all applicants, including receptionists and dock workers. When he was not consulted before an offer was made, he would rescind the offer. While no litigation was initiated, he succeeded in losing the respect of most everyone in the organization. His intent may have been sincere, but the result was sad.

You have to let go at some point. The key to a smooth transition is adequate training of all involved.

14. If you have delegated hiring tasks to others, have they been properly trained to handle the responsibility?

Too often, a supervisor is given permission to fill a vacant position and has little or no training to do so. This is where much litigation arises. Everyone having hiring power or influence should be properly trained for the task. The initial investment is outweighed by the savings in lost time, turnover and legal considerations. Consider the employee selection training outline on this page.

Employee Selection Training Session

September 1, 1997
7:30-10:30 AM

OUTLINE

I. Employment Law
    A. Laws to be aware of
    B. What you can or cannot say or do
    C. Common Pitfalls

II. Reviewing Resumes and Applications
    A. What to look for
    B. Common applicant "tricks"

III. How to Check References
    A. What to ask
    B. How to ask
    C. How to read a reference

BREAK

IV. Interviews
    A. What to ask
    B. What to look for
    C. Pointers to conducting an interview

V. Making the Decision
    A. What to evaluate
    B. How to compare

VI. Recordkeeping
    A. Records we must keep
    B. What you may ask after the person has been hired

---

15. Have you checked on your competitors to discover their secrets of hiring?

What are other organizations doing to assure optimum hiring? There is usually an abundance of information available (such as this book) to gather ideas for improving your system. Check with trade associations, chambers of commerce, and libraries for the latest information on salary data.

16. How "user friendly" is the overall hiring system? Could anyone understand it?

There are many unwritten laws in most organizations about who has influence over what function. This type of authority should be clearly defined to insure consistency and accuracy. Written procedures should be developed for all hiring, and these documents should be updated as needed.

This does not have to be a manual three feet thick. Investing the short amount of time it takes to prepare a document like this, will eliminate hours of questions later.

II. Alternatives to Recruiting

Hiring new employees may not always be the best way to go. More than one employer has experienced the frustration of recruiting new people only to let them go six months later when the business slowed down. An uptick in sales is not necessarily long term.

In addition, some organizations choose to staff with their ranks with people contracted in a variety of ways. They can be divided into four categories:

- Temporary employees
- Contracted managers and professionals
- Job shops
- Leased labor

Temporary Employees

The traditional idea of a "temp" is one who fills in for the receptionist when she's sick. This practice has radically changed and expanded over the past few years. Temporary help can be found in all departments within a company, performing all sorts of work.

Employing temporaries in place of full-timers offers several advantages:

> **Selecting a Temporary Service**
>
> Is it a member of the National Association of Temporary Services?
>
> Does it adhere to NAT's code of ethics?
>
> Does it have a formal policy on evaluating each temp's assignment?
>
> Does it provide temps with instruction on office equipment?
>
> Can it provide references from other clients?
>
> Does it check references and background on the people it provides?
>
> Does it have a professional staff that develops client relationships so they know your needs?
>
> Does it have a formal contract you can take away and have reviewed by an attorney?

- It provides the needed staff assistance without the burden of benefits.
- There are fewer layoffs involved especially in seasonal businesses.

- It offers an opportunity to try out employees whose qualifications may be borderline for a full-time position.
- There is less of a personnel paper trail since the person is not working for you, but for the agency.
- Discipline problems can be resolved by asking that the temporary be replaced.
- These individuals are already screened for necessary qualifications and experience.

The disadvantages can be lack of training, little investment in the organization, and a constant turnover of new faces which can influence morale. Costs must be watched carefully since a disorganized use of temporaries can be more expensive than hiring full-time staff.

How to Access Temporaries

In addition to the listing of temporary services in the phone book, you might contact the local chapter of the National Association of Temporary Services (703-549-6287) or the Association of Part-time Professionals (703-734-7975). Ask plenty of questions of these services. What to ask? Check the table on page 10.

Contracted Managers and Professionals

The concept of contracted managers and professionals has grown in popularity as organizations are increasingly cautious about hiring full-timers. Only in existence for the past five years, companies offering this service provide a professional that assumes a particular role within the organization for a defined period of time.

The contracting organization pays the agency and the agency pays the professional. This concept offers several advantages:

- These professionals can be contracted for a day, week, month or more.
- They generally have at least ten years' experience in their field of expertise.
- They can be paid as contractors, eliminating costly paperwork.
- The agency brings qualified candidates to you, eliminating the search.

- The agency will, if asked, help coordinate the project or responsibilities
- You retain supervisory control.
- This is a great way to "try before you buy" when hiring for critical positions

How to Access Contracted Employees

Agencies handling contracted professionals are few in number at present, but starting in many cities. To locate them you might check with the local chamber of commerce or with a chapter of the American Society for Personnel Administrators.

Another alternative is to consult local professional organizations in the area of expertise you seek. If they are not aware of a service like this, some members might be interested in making an arrangement on their own.

Job Shops

Job shops are temporary help agencies that specialize in specific tasks. A good example of this would be so called "letter shops" which handle direct mail for catalog distributors. Rather than hiring individuals to stuff and seal envelopes, the distributor contracts with a letter shop who handle the entire process. This eliminates the employer's recruiting, training and payroll processes.

In professional areas, job shops can provide everyone from accountants to systems analysts, to engineers. These individuals serve on long- or short-term assignments.

For certain, defined projects this alternative may represent significant cost savings along with time and effort.

How to Access Job Shops

Jobs shops are located in every city. To locate them look up the type of industry or service you need in the Yellow Pages. You might also check with trade or professional associations for recommendations and additional ideas on how to work with these agencies.

Employee Leasing

Staff leasing is a relatively new concept. After you have contracted with one of these organizations, your employees are discharged, and hired by this firm and then leased back to your organization. Everyone retains their original position. You retain supervisory control, but the leasing company is now the employer.

The leasing company issues paychecks, provides benefits, and handles the necessary paperwork normally maintained by a personnel department. Hiring, firing, and discipline are a joint effort.

A major advantage of leasing employees is better benefits and human resources management for your staff. Since a leasing firm may be handling thousands of employees, it can take advantage of large group insurance discounts to which a smaller organization does not have access.

The downside of this strategy is lack of continuity and loyalty. With their new found relationship, employees may not stay in one company as long, moving from lessee to lessee. Additionally, pension legislation has complicated the process for employers using this service by adding special paperwork and compliance.

How to Access Leasing Companies

Since employee leasing is not widespread, the best means for locating these services is through the National Staff Leasing Association or the American Society for Personnel Administrators. Once again, ask plenty of questions before proceeding since leasing employees will have a major impact on your staff relations.

Where Do We Go from Here?

The checklist above should give you a working knowledge of the considerations necessary to conduct an effective employee selection program. The next chapter covers the myriad of laws and regulations surrounding employee selection. Be sure to examine this information thoroughly since significant portions of it have changed in the past five years.

The Legal Requirements of Hiring

"My client says he took one look around your company and realized there were nothing but whites," said the attorney. "He says he's perfect for the job and that you rejected him because he's Hispanic."

"That's not true!" insisted the owner. "We hire anybody who's qualified for the job."

"I hope you can prove that in court," retorted the lawyer.

Here's What You'll Learn

I.   What Laws Apply
II. Common Selection Issues
III. Negligent Hiring
IV. Enforcement and Recordkeeping
V.   State Requirements
VI. A Checklist for Hiring Law

Twenty thousand dollars!! That's how much the American Bar Association has estimated it costs in legal fees alone to defend a discrimination lawsuit that goes to trial.

In this litigious society, the need for a solid knowledge of employment law has become crucial for managers. In addition to the myriad of federal laws, each state maintains its own collection of statutes.

Federal, state, and local labor laws have been enacted to protect those living in the United States from discrimination in hiring. There are currently over 400 federal laws pertaining to employee rights and selection. While it would be counterproductive to address each and every one in this chapter, the major laws and applications will be covered. It is highly recommended that a competent employment attorney be consulted regarding the idiosyncrasies of the laws in your area.

I. What Laws Apply

The Civil Rights Act of 1964 is the cornerstone to antidiscrimination legislation in the United States. Title VII of this act pertains to labor and employment. Its purpose is to require the removal of artificial, arbitrary, and unnecessary barriers to employment when such impediments discriminate against individuals on the basis of race, sex, or religious beliefs.

Executive Orders 11246 and 11375 require federal contractors with $50,000 in contracts and 50 or more employees to develop affirmative action programs to ensure equal opportunity. These orders also established the Office of Federal Contract Compliance Programs (OFCCP) to enforce these orders.

The Pregnancy Discrimination Act of 1978 amended Title VII to prohibit discrimination on the basis of childbirth, pregnancy or related medical conditions.

The Age Discrimination in Employment Act (as amended in 1978) prohibits discrimination in hiring of individuals age 40 and older.

The Vocational Rehabilitation Act of 1973 prohibits job discrimination against otherwise qualified disabled individuals. This statute applies to all employers with federal contracts in excess of $2500 or that receive financial assistance from the federal government.

The Vietnam Era Veterans' Readjustment Assistance Act of 1974 requires that all employers with federal contracts of $10,000 or more take affirmative action to employ and advance disabled veterans and qualified veterans of the Vietnam era. Administered by OFCCP.

The Immigration Reform and Control Act of 1986 prohibits the employment of illegal aliens, except under certain specified conditions.

The Fair Labor Standards Act, as amended by the **Equal Pay Act,** sets minimum wages, as well as overtime and equal pay standards.

The Polygraph Protection Act of 1988 prohibits the use of polygraphs and voice print devices with certain exceptions.

The Americans with Disabilities Act of 1990 prohibits discrimination against qualified individuals with disabilities in employment, public services, transportation, public accommodation, and telecommunications.

The Civil Rights Act of 1991 reestablishes the burden of proof on the employer to prove business necessity during a discrimination complaint filed by an applicant or employee. In addition, it provides for monetary damages and the right to a jury trial in these cases. Finally, it says that test scores cannot be adjusted to alter the results of employment related tests on the basis of race, color, religion, sex or national origin. This forbids employers from "boosting" the scores of those in protected classes for the purpose of artificially enhancing the organization's affirmative action efforts.

Who Is Affected

Title VII and the Americans with Disabilities Act apply to all private employers, the federal state and local governments, educational institutions and labor organizations that have fifteen or more employees. These same parameters apply to the Age Discrimination in Employment Act and the Pregnancy Discrimination Act of 1978.

The exception to these guidelines is the Immigration Reform and Control Act (IRCA). Under this legislation, all newly hired employees are required to show proof of their eligibility to work in the United States within the first three days of employment. Unlike Title VII and other antidiscrimination laws, IRCA includes all employers.

If you hire a housekeeper for example, that person must show proof of eligibility to work in the United States.

In addition to the federal government, many states have passed laws governing employment that parallel federal legislation. Since state laws are often broader, more comprehensive, and stringent than federal statutes, it is paramount that those performing the hiring function be familiar with these laws. The most stringent law, whether federal, state or local, is the one that applies.

Equal Employment Opportunity Commission (www.eeoc.gov)

The Equal Employment Opportunity Commission (EEOC) was created to enforce Title VII of the Civil Rights Act of 1964. In addition, it currently enforces the Pregnancy Discrimination Act, the Age Discrimination in Employment Act, the Equal Pay Act and the Americans with Disabilities Act, and the Civil Rights Act of 1991.

The commission consists of five members who are appointed by the President with the advice and consent of the United States Senate. The EEOC has established district offices throughout the nation and collects and publishes data on discriminatory practices in addition to investigating violations of employees' civil rights.

The Vocational Rehabilitation Act of 1973 and Executive Orders 11375 and 11246 are enforced by the Office of Federal Contract Compliance Programs and each federal agency. The Immigration Reform and Control Act is enforced by the Immigration and Naturalization Service although the law is written so that employers are each responsible for enforcement within their own companies.

Selection Guidelines

To assist employers in abiding by the federal antidiscrimination laws, the Equal Employment Opportunity Commission developed the *Uniform Guidelines for Employee Selection Procedures* in 1978. The purpose of these guidelines is to help those hiring employees to interpret the federal statutes. It is not the questions asked by an employer that are unlawful. It is what the employer might do with the answers that comes into question.

It is perfectly legal, for example, to ask a question like "That's an interesting accent. Where did you grow up?" However the employer must realize that the question infers that the applicant's nationality is of concern in the hiring process. Unless there is job-related reason, this question could lead to charges of discrimination. Even if there is a legitimate reason, such as a U.S. Defense Department requirement, the correct question is "Are you a U.S. citizen?"

Bona Fide Occupational Qualifications

In certain instances, an employer will have a legitimate reason for setting standards that restrict the hiring of particular groups. A warehouse job for example, may require individuals hired be able to lift seventy-five pounds. This may appear outwardly discriminatory toward women. If this requirement can be demonstrated to be a "business necessity" however, it will be considered a bona fide occupational qualification (BFOQ). BFOQ's have been narrowly interpreted by the courts and are a rare form of defense in a discrimination suit.

Sample EEO-1 Form

The best advice concerning exceptions to the antidiscrimination laws is to assume there are no exceptions. Approach each hiring requirement as if all individuals are eligible regardless of age, sex, race, religion, national origin, disability, and marital status.

Adverse Impact

Under Title VII of the Civil Rights Act of 1964, an employer's hiring practices become illegal when the company operates to the disadvantage of one or more protected classes of individuals. While the employment practices may be neutral in appearance and intent, the company's hiring practices must reflect the characteristics of the surrounding community. If, for example, a company's selection process rejected a disproportionate number of blacks at compared to whites, then the company would be guilty of adverse impact. In the landmark case Griggs vs. Duke Power Company, the power company required all applicants to pass a math test as part of the selection process. Investigation of the complaint revealed that a disproportionate number of blacks failed the test. Since Mr. Griggs was applying for a custodial job, where math was not required, the test was found to have an adverse impact on his protected class.

There are a number of variables entering into this equation such as the ratios of existing employees within the organization and the population of certain protected classes within the surrounding community. It is best to keep accurate records of hiring patterns no matter what your company's size.

Affirmative Action Requirements

If a company is found to be in violation of Title VII statutes by the EEOC or courts, it may be required to establish an affirmative action plan to integrate its work force. This action may require the employer to hire applicants from protected classes, and to recruit them if insufficient numbers apply.

> ### Key Components of Affirmative Action
>
> An employer is not required to establish an affirmative action plan unless it has shown discrimination in the past. (The exceptions to this are federal contractors with $50,000 in federal work and more than 50 employees.)
>
> There must be a clear assignment of direction for the program.
>
> The plan must contain clearly stated procedures.
>
> The plan must contain a clearly stated equal opportunity policy.
>
> The plan must contain specific goals and timetables for hiring protected groups who are under-represented.

Employers working under federal contract rules have even more stringent requirements. Under Presidential Executive Orders 11246 and 11375, all employers with more than $50,000 in federal contracts and 50 or more employees are required to establish affirmative action plans regardless of whether they have been forced to do so because of adverse impact. The executive orders take precedence over Title VII legislation.

In addition, employers with more than $10,000 in federal contracts are required to establish an affirmative action program for qualified Vietnam-era veterans under the Vietnam-era Veterans Adjustment Act of 1974. Failure to do so can result in loss of eligibility for federal contracts.

II. Common Selection Issues

Job relatedness is the key determinant in deciding whether a particular requirement can be considered a hiring condition. Job requirements that have a disparate impact on certain protected classes are prohibited by the federal government and most states. Some of the more common job requirements and their allowances are listed below:

Accents: Candidates may be excluded from a position if that position requires substantial communication between customers and/or employees and the person's accent is found to be so great that it would impair that person's performance.

Age requirements: Employment discrimination due to age is prohibited under the Age Discrimination in Employment Act of 1967 (as amended in 1978) except in situations where there is a bona fide occupational qualification. Other statutory exceptions, such as the positions of airline pilot and senior corporate executive are also made.

Employment of aliens: The Immigration Reform and Control Act along with many state statutes prohibit the hiring of aliens unless they have obtained permission to work in the United States. It is now an employer's legal responsibility to check an employee's working status within three days of hire.

Alienage: It is unlawful, according to Title VII, to require citizenship as a standard for hire if the result is discrimination against individuals on the basis of national origin. The major reasons for requiring citizenship usually center around national security.

Appearance and dress: An employer may not reject an applicant for employment on the basis of appearance and dress if that appearance and dress is typical of that applicant's culture. However an employer may set standards of dress if these are substantially related to the employer's needs. Common reasons for this would be safety and commonly accepted social norms. Some locales have passed ordinances prohibiting discrimination because of personal appearance, especially related to religious custom.

Arrest and criminal records: The EEOC prohibits the requirement that applicants have no previous arrest record. It is also unlawful to reject an applicant on the basis of conviction of a crime unless that crime was substantially related to job responsibilities. An applicant who has been convicted of embezzlement, for example, could be refused a job as a bookkeeper.

An employer can also ask about pending indictments since the answer can be relevant to job performance. One of these factors would be crimes related to the job such as an indictment for embezzlement in a cashiers position, or a charge of theft for a warehouse supervisor. Another factor would be the length of time the person may need to pursue his/her defense.

Blacklisting: It is unlawful, in most states, to maintain a "blacklist" of applicants for any reason.

Credit requirement: It is against EEOC guidelines to require a good credit rating as a condition of employment unless the employer can demonstrate business necessity. This is a reasonable qualification, for example, in the hiring of a credit manager or cashier.

Dependents' status: Employers are prohibited from rejecting a female applicant because she has children of pre-school age when no such requirement exists for male applicants. Nor can she be refused because she is an unwed mother since this condition has no relation to business necessity.

Disability: As of July 26, 1992 employers with 25 or more employees will be subject to the Americans with Disabilities Act of 1990 (ADA). ADA requirements mirror those of the Vocational Rehabilitation Act. Employers with 15 or more employees are subject to this act.

The courts have held that disabilities are not limited to physical conditions. They may also include suicidal tendencies, a borderline personality, post traumatic stress syndrome and other conditions as yet undetermined. Alcoholics and drug addicts are also considered disabled if their condition currently prevents them from performing a job adequately. Both must in the recovery stages.

Employers are also subject to the Vocational Rehabilitation Act of 1973 if they receive grants from the federal government or have federal contracts in excess of $2500 annually. Under this Act, an employer is required to provide reasonable accommodation to disabled applicants. This may include wheelchair access, removal of architectural barriers, adjustments of furniture and equipment, and special aids for telephones.

Education: An employer may use education as a requirement only to the extent where the education can be demonstrated to be a business necessity. A high school diploma, for example, cannot be used as a condition of employment unless it can be shown that the skills provided in a high school education are substantially related to job duties.

Fingerprinting: The fingerprinting of employees is generally accepted in all states with the exception of New York where authority to do so is limited.

Hair requirement: It is generally considered a violation of Title VII to have a hair requirement that differs from men to women. However it has not been a major issue in the courts as long as there has been no disparate impact on either sex.

Health requirements: An applicant may be refused employment if s/he fails a physical examination as long as the requirements in the exam demonstrate that the applicant would not be able to perform on the job. For example, an employer can reject an applicant for an electronics assembly position who fails a coordination test. It is important to remember that all physicals should be given after a contingent offer has been made. This eliminates concern about violating the Americans with Disabilities Act.

Height/weight requirement: Applicants protected by Title VII can be refused employment on the basis of a height or weight requirement provided the employer demonstrates job relatedness. An applicant who is 6'5" tall for example, may be refused a flight attendant position due to safety restrictions.

Language requirement: Proficiency in English may not be required as a condition for employment under Title VII due to disparate impact unless the employer can demonstrate business necessity. A retail clerk, for example, can be required to be proficient in English.

Marital status: An employer may not have a policy prohibiting the hiring of married women unless this same policy prohibits the hiring of married men.

Military record: Unless the employer can demonstrate that the decision was related to job performance, an applicant may not be rejected on the basis of having received a less-than-honorable discharge from the military.

National origin: Unless a bona fide occupational qualification has been established, an applicant may not be rejected on the basis of national origin.

Nepotism: An employer's policy of prohibiting nepotism may be in violation of Title VII if it has a disparate impact on a protected class. In a small town, for example, a company's prohibition on nepotism may have a disparate impact on women due to the number of jobs available in the community. This same adverse impact might exist in a community with a large minority population.

Polygraph/lie detector: As of January 1, 1989, private sector employers are prohibited from using polygraphs, voice print devices and other related technologies in the selection of employees. The three major exceptions to this law are certain defense, security or pharmaceutical-related jobs. (See Chapter Ten for a more complete discussion.)

Pregnancy: The Pregnancy Discrimination Act of 1978 (Title VII) prohibits discrimination against women affected by pregnancy, childbirth and related medical conditions.

Recruitment: There are no specific prohibitions concerning the recruitment of certain applicants. However, an employer who grants preferential treatment to friends and relatives may be in violation of Title VII guidelines if one or more protected classes are under-represented in the firm. This also holds true concerning referrals from other company employees.

Religious conviction: Employers must make reasonable accommodation to an applicant's religious convictions and may not reject them on that basis unless it would create undue hardship on the employer's business. An applicant should not suffer in being considered for a job, for example, because s/he asks that an interview be moved due to the observance of a religious holiday.

Sexual orientation: Currently, there is no federal legislation covering sexual orientation. Some locales however have passed law addressing these issues.

Sexual status: An employer may not limit a job to "females only" or "males only" unless a bona fide occupational qualification is evident. An example of this might be the role of a male or female character in a theatrical production.

No-spouse requirement: It is lawful to have a rule prohibiting the hiring of a spouse as long as the rule is neutral. In other words, if the wife of a male employee cannot be hired, the husband of a female employee cannot be hired.

Strength requirement: An employer can require that applicants pass a strength test provided the requirement is a business necessity. A stocking position in a warehouse, for example, could have a lawful strength requirement if the employer can demonstrate its legitimacy.

Testing (aptitude/psychological): The requirement that applicants submit to aptitude or psychological testing is unlawful unless the employer can demonstrate relatedness to job performance. In all cases, the tests are subject to validation by the EEOC. In addition, they must not have an unequal impact on protected classes. (See Chapter Ten for additional information.)

Testing (drugs): There are several debates revolving around the legal use of pre-employment drug testing. These include accuracy, invasion of privacy and relatedness to job performance. It is best to tread carefully in this area. (A full discussion of this topic can be found in Chapter Ten.)

Work experience: An employer may require previous work experience provided that relatedness and business necessity can be demonstrated. The amount required must be reasonable according to the job duties. For example, a grocery cashier's position requiring two years' experience is unreasonable.

III. Negligent Hiring

A new concern for employers is the expanding concept of negligent hiring. Under this theory, employers who know or should have known that an employee is unfit for a position may be liable for the employee's criminal or tortuous behavior. Negligent hiring is now recognized as a "cause of action" in more than 30 states.

Generally, an employer has a duty to exercise reasonable care when hiring employees who, if incompetent or unreliable, might cause a risk of injury to the public or fellow employees by reason of their employment. Examples of this theory have been illustrated by court cases such as an employee who used a pass key to enter an apartment and attack a tenant and a taxi driver who raped a rider in his cab.

A plaintiff has to prove three things in negligent hiring cases: 1) that the employee who caused the injury was unfit for hiring or retention. 2) The employer's hiring or retention of the unfit employee was the cause of the plaintiff's injuries. 3) The employer knew, or should have known, the unfitness.

To protect against negligent hiring, several steps should be applied in screening candidates. These steps include:

- Review applicable federal state and local laws to ensure your process conforms to all such laws.
- Comply with federal, state and local fair credit reporting laws if a credit check is conducted.
- Look for gaps in employment and other suspicious or unusual entries in candidates' applications.
- Calling each reference listed on the application.
- Obtain a signed waiver and consent form from each applicant to conduct a full reference check.
- Document all information received, including licenses, diplomas, and certificates, as well as efforts to obtain this information if it was not available.
- Require all employees who have served in the armed forces to provide a copy of their DD-214 stating they were discharged honorably.

- Decide whether it is appropriate to conduct a criminal records search in view of the job being filled.
- Carefully review the background and experience of the applicants for jobs that involve public safety, the operation of motor vehicles, aircraft, trains and the like.
- Do not offer employment until screening and testing has been completed.
- If appropriate, require a physical examination of the applicant. Make sure the applicant consents to the examination.
- Even if an employee is transferring within the organization, reexamine his/her fitness for the new position.

IV. Enforcement and Recordkeeping

The federal government has detailed specific procedures and remedies for failure to comply with the guidelines for anti-discrimination under Title VII, the Pregnancy Discrimination Act, the Age Discrimination in Employment Act, the Rehabilitation Act, the Americans with Disabilities Act and the Immigration Reform and Control Act. The Equal Employment Opportunity Commission is responsible for enforcement of all except the IRCA.

Procedures

If an applicant feels s/he has been the victim of discrimination in a company's hiring process, that person may choose to file a complaint with the Equal Employment Opportunity Commission along with state and local authorities. A claimant has 180 days from the day of the action to file a complaint with the EEOC. If the state or locale in which the discrimination allegedly took place has its own anti-discrimination laws, then federal guidelines allow a filing time of 300 days. This extension is allowed to give the state or locale ample time to act on the complaint.

After the investigation has been completed, the commission will issue a determination that either no discrimination took place or discrimination did take place. If the commission finds that no discrimination took place, it will issue a "right-to-sue" notice to the claimant explaining that the claimant may still pursue this matter in district court.

If discrimination is found, both parties will be invited by the commission to join in a conciliation process. An EEOC conciliator will attempt to get the two parties to come to an agreement regarding the alleged discrimination. If the respondent (company) refuses to enter into conciliation or the parties fail to come to an agreement, the EEOC will terminate the proceedings and issue another "right-to-sue" notice to the claimant.

Under certain circumstances the EEOC itself may bring suits against companies it feels are engaged in a pattern of discrimination. It may also enforce the Title VII conciliation agreement in district court if it believes the respondent is not performing.

Remedies

With the enactment of Civil Rights Act of 1991, the remedies for violating the myriad of federal discrimination laws (including sexual harassment) increased in their severity. This new act provides for both compensatory and punitive damages along with jury trials for employees who are claiming intentional discrimination.

The remedies for these judgments are varied and depend upon the severity of discrimination. A main determinant is the employer's intention at the time the act took place. Where the action is blatant, as in a rule such as, "no women need apply," the remedies are apt to be severe.

In a situation where the employer is guilty of disparate treatment, the remedies may be less severe. Disparate treatment can be described as discrimination as the result of neutral hiring rules. If, for example, an employer has been advertising for laborers and the requirements listed could be construed as male when a female could perform the job, then discrimination may result.

Once an employer has been found libel of discrimination, a number of reliefs may be made to the plaintiff. These include the hiring of individuals who have successfully sued for discrimination, allotment of back pay with interest, attorneys' fees, health and disability benefits, and retroactive seniority and pension benefits.

Employers may also be required to locate past victims of bias. In some cases, hiring goals and ratios are established to make up for past inequities. Finally, as mentioned above, monetary damages may be awarded.

Defenses to Title VII and the Age Discrimination Act

There are several typical defenses that employers can use for Title VII claims. The most prevalent of these is business necessity. In this situation, the court will look at legitimate business purpose and whether there is truly no alternative policy or practice.

A second defense is a jurisdictional defect in the plaintiff's claim. The most common of these is failure to file within the prescribed period (180 days).

A third is a bona fide occupational qualification. The courts have severely limited these defenses.

Classifying Exempt and Nonexempt Employees
Fair Labor Standards Act - 1936

Exempt employees are determined by two factors:
1. Duties and responsibilities
2. Salary Paid

Each person must meet all of the criteria in their category below:

	Executive	Administrative	Professional	Outside Sales
Primary Duties	Manager of the enterprise or a subsidiary. Customarily supervises at least two. Authority to hire/fire.	Non-manual work directly related to policy making and operations. Duties related to education or training. Customarily exercises independent judgement and authority.	Specialized knowledge requiring instruction or Original and creative work in an artistic field or Certified or recognized instructor Customarily exercises discretion and judgement	Customarily works away from place of business selling or taking orders.
Time Requirement	20% of time can be spent on non-managerial duties, 40% in service or retail.	20% of time can be spent on non-manage-rial duties, 40% in service or retail.	20% of time can be spent on non-professional duties.	20% of time can be spent doing work normally performed by non-exempt employees.
Salary Requirement	Minimum of $155/wk other than room and board. At $250/wk, 20% rule changes to majority of time must be spent on management.	Minimum of $155/wk other than room and board. At $250/wk, 20% rule changes to majority of time must be spent on administrative duties.	At least $170/week other than room and board. At $250/wk, 20% rule changes to majority of time must be spent on professional duties.	NONE

Other defenses include seniority systems, testing that demonstrates the employer's reasoning for action, and reasonable accommodation in which the employer made an attempt to address the applicant's situation.

Typical defenses to age discrimination are legitimate seniority systems, bona fide occupational qualifications and rejection on the basis of other factors not involving age.

The Equal Pay Act of 1963

Although the Equal Pay Act of 1963 does not apply to hiring practices per se, *all employers* should make sure their compensation policies treat all employees equally. A violation of this act may be triggered by the hiring of a new employee with compensation inequitable to others who are doing comparable work with comparable experience.

The Fair Labor Standards Act exempts employees from hourly pay regulations provided they meet certain requirements concerning duties, responsibilities, and salary paid.

Recordkeeping

The Equal Employment Opportunity Commission requires all employers falling under the jurisdiction of Title VII to preserve employment records for a period of six months. This includes application forms and all other data relating to the hiring process. This six month period begins on the day the record was made and/or the personnel action was taken.

Employment records relevant to any charge of discrimination must be kept until the disposition of the complaint or litigation.

Recordkeeping that pertains to the Age Discrimination in Employment Act requires employers to preserve all materials relating to the hiring process for one year from date of action or record being made. The Equal Pay Act requires all employers to maintain and preserve wage and compensation records for two years. *The bottom line is that employment records should be kept for one year and compensation records should be kept for two.*

To ease your understanding of these laws, a matrix detailing the requirements can be found in Appendix B.

V. State Requirements

State laws regarding equal employment are generally broader in scope than federal statutes. With the exception of Alabama, all states now have laws protecting certain classes of individuals in the employment process. Employers must comply with all state and federal laws affecting their locale.

It is critical for employers to be aware of all state employment laws that affect the hiring process. While the federal government, for instance, does not enforce Title VII until an employer has reached fifteen employees, individual state laws may be triggered with a lesser number. In fact, laws in thirteen states and the District of Columbia provide that employers are subject to the state's statutes if they employ one or more people. Other states define employers that employ two or more to twenty-five or more.

Some local ordinances provide additional protection to certain individuals. These generally include, homosexuals, the handicapped and those with Acquired Immune Deficiency Syndrome (AIDS). Check with your attorney to be sure you are within the local laws.

Be aware of more restrictive rules in recruiting, interviewing, testing, and use of applications. In an Ohio study, ninety-four applications were collected for analysis. Seventy-three percent were found to contain at least one illegal pre-employment inquiry according to state law.

Although all complaints must be filed with the Equal Employment Opportunity Commission in addition to the state agency, EEOC defers investigation to the state for sixty days. After that time, its jurisdiction to investigate returns unless the state agency has begun an investigation. In that case, the EEOC will wait for the outcome of that inquiry.

The states follow procedures that parallel those of the federal agency. In fact, the EEOC has a written agreement with each state concerning these practices.

While the state laws can vary, there are several excellent references available to assist you in understanding your company's obligations.

VI. A Checklist for Hiring Law

_____1.   Have you developed a strong working knowledge of:
Title VII of the Civil Rights Act of 1964
Age Discrimination in Employment Act
Americans with Disabilities Act
Equal Pay Act (pertaining to hiring)
Pregnancy Discrimination Act of 1978
Vocational Rehabilitation Act of 1973
Civil Rights Act of 1991

_____2.   Can you explain affirmative action and adverse impact?

_____3.   Can you explain a bona fide occupational qualification?

_____4.   Have you developed a working knowledge of the applicable employment laws in all states in which the company operates?

_____5.   Can you explain the laws and decisions regarding the job relatedness of the following:

_____Education	_____Health requirements
_____Strength requirement	_____Height/weight requirement
_____Work experience	_____Appearance and dress
_____Hair requirement	_____Credit requirement
_____Alienage	_____Arrest and criminal records
_____Military record	_____No-spouse requirement
_____Language requirement	_____Dependents' status
_____Marital status	_____Sex status
_____Pregnancy	_____National origin
_____Religious convictions	_____Handicap
_____Age requirements	_____Sexual Harassment
_____Nepotism	

Job Descriptions and Compensation

The applicant asked for a written job description.

"We don't have it written down," responded the owner. "But let me tell you what the person does."

"Are you telling me what the person does or what they're supposed to do?" she asked.

"Jobs evolve," said the owner, "all I can give you is a rough sketch."

"So you really don't know what you're hiring for," she said.

Here's What You'll Learn

I.	Importance of Job Descriptions
II.	Job Analysis and Audit
III.	Writing Job Descriptions
IV.	Determining Compensation
V.	A Checklist for Job Descriptions and Compensation

I. Importance of Job Descriptions

Most Americans have never seen a written description for their job. The average company cannot provide written job descriptions for all existing positions.

The analysis of jobs and writing of descriptions is tedious. Yet it provides an excellent opportunity to define the exact requirements for each job. As a company grows, positions may be added without much thought to the design of duties.

This evolution tends to be haphazard and disorganized. When a position needs to be filled, no one seems to know *exactly* what the incumbent did.

A job description provides definition and focus. Parameters within which the person will work are identified. It describes day-to-day responsibilities, levels of authority, and the person to whom the new employee reports.

A job description can be used in a variety of ways. For the purposes of hiring, it:

1. assists in explaining the job to applicants,
2. serves as a basis for writing job postings, and developing a list of criteria for a successful candidate to meet.

After the person has been hired, it:

1. gives the new employee a direction and basis from which to start,
2. serves as a tool in the measurement of performance.

Some people view a job description as limiting. It may hinder their creativity by setting defined boundaries. Those holding the position might be hesitant to step beyond its scope. Employees with brilliant ideas for instance, may bury them because they believe they will be told to stick to the job at hand.

Consider the position of office manager. While the duties may be straightforward, you also want to encourage this individual to use creativity in solving daily problems. Outlining too many job specifications will work against you.

On the other hand, it is hard to get some workers to do the job assigned, let alone granting authority to wander. A balance has to be developed between defining the job and welcoming creativity. Encouraging a dock foreman to think creatively while loading trucks may end in more bureaucracy than productivity.

In some cases, job descriptions are being enhanced by video tapes of employees at work to show applicants what jobs are really like.

Current employees are taped at work and asked to talk about their day-to-day duties and responsibilities, the most rewarding and stressful aspects of their jobs and why they like working for the organization. These videos are featured at job fairs and other recruiting events.

A final consideration is that of potential litigation. While there are no specific legal requirements for having these documents, organizations unable to produce descriptions of jobs in question face an uphill battle in wrongful discharge and discrimination suits.

The enactment of the Americans with Disabilities Act has made job descriptions a higher priority than in the past. The Equal Employment Opportunity Commission has made it clear that job descriptions will be used as the basis for initial determination during the investigation of an ADA complaint. These descriptions should be in place during the hiring process, not just for the purposes of dealing with addressing legal requirements.

Do You Need the Job?

Before proceeding with the development of a job description, determine whether the position is actually necessary. In the rush of new found business or expansion, it is easy to imagine the need for a new person to assume some of the responsibility. On the other hand, this same person may be unnecessary six months hence when business slows. While the work may overload existing employees for the moment, be careful not to create a new position that will have to be eliminated later. Consider the questions to the left.

Once you have decided there is justification for creating this position, the next step is to analyze the actual needs and functions.

II. Job Analysis and Audit

Before a job description can be developed, an analysis of the position, existing or proposed, must be conducted. While this can be involved, it does not have to be. The key is to ask the right questions. All job audits should answer the eight questions at right.

Audits should be performed for existing jobs in addition to those newly created. Turnover is an unpredictable creature. The occupied position today may be the vacancy of tomorrow.

Clear communication is essential while conducting a job audit. Anytime someone starts "inspecting" jobs, rumors will abound, even in a small company. A short memo or mention at a staff meeting should quell concern.

Existing Jobs

To properly audit an existing job, you must first develop a questionnaire covering the general categories of work. It might be designed in the manner of the example on the following page.

Anyone can perform the analysis, although it is not a good idea to have the present jobholder do so. This person may tend to exaggerate the responsibilities. It is better to have an objective staff member interview the job holder and record the information.

The descriptions in an audit should be specific and measured. A duty such as "takes care of all the inventory paperwork," is not acceptable.

A better way of relating the same thing might be:

"Is responsible for the completion of all paperwork on incoming inventory. This includes, but is not limited to, checking manifests against actual counts, recording and assigning storage for all incoming freight,

---

Do You Need the Job?

1. What is the purpose of this new job?

2. Who is presently performing these tasks?

3. How long have the employees who presently perform these tasks been overloaded?

4. Is this added business the result of a cycle or is the pace more permanent?

5. What will be the initial goals of this position and how long will it take to accomplish them?

6. What is the best that can happen if we fill this position with a good person?

7. Is there enough work for a full-time position? Can it be performed by a part-time employee?

8. Can some of the overload duties be switched to another area within the same department or location?

9. Is this a true need or can the systems in this function be streamlined for better productivity?

10. How much will this new position cost?

11. Is there a sufficient labor market to choose from?

12. Will this position exist 24 months from now?

13. Have you checked with all the parties involved to determine if everyone feels there is a need?

14. How will other departments view adding this new position?

15. What impact will the creation of this new position have on the jobs from which the tasks are being removed?

16. What is the worst that can happen if we don't create this position?

Job Audit Questions

1. What duties does the person perform to complete the job? (Be specific in description.)

2. What tools, services and/or accommodations does the person need to complete these duties?

3. Who supervises the person in this position?

4. With which other people does this person interact, both in and out of the organization?

5. Is the person performing the job able to complete all duties in the time allotted?

6. What formal training does a person need to perform this job, if any?

7. What skills does the person need to complete this job? (Include technical, interpersonal, organizational, and problem-solving skills.

8. How is the person performing this job evaluated?

```
┌─────────────────────────────────────────┐
│              Job Audit                   │
│                                          │
│  Audit conducted by_____ Date____ │
│                                          │
│  Job title_____  │
│                                          │
│  Major duties:                           │
│                                          │
│  Minor duties:                           │
│                                          │
│                                          │
│  Is supervised by (state relation):      │
│                                          │
│  Number of employees supervised (state relation): │
│                                          │
│  Training required:                      │
│                                          │
│  Education required:                     │
│                                          │
│  Certificates/licenses required:         │
│                                          │
│  Experience required (identify specific skills): │
│                                          │
│  Physical requirements:                  │
│                                          │
│  On-the-job hazards/working conditions:  │
│                                          │
│  Source of job audit information:        │
│                                          │
└─────────────────────────────────────────┘
```

maintaining accurate control over all internal distribution of inventory. This responsibility entails 60% of average weekly time."

While the second description is more involved, it is also more accurate and gives the readers a realistic picture of what the job entails. Since responsibilities change on a constant basis, it is best to reassess all job descriptions on a periodic basis.

A completed job audit form can be found on page 38. Note the informality and easy to read descriptions.

New Jobs

While it is impossible to determine the actual duties in a newly created job, you can usually make an accurate estimation. The same questions asked about an existing job need to be asked in this case.

The process is best performed by the person who will supervise the position. It may then be reviewed by others for modifications and corrections. Before proceeding, ask whether the job is "do-able." While the amount of time necessary to complete the new job cannot be thoroughly determined, one should be careful not to overload the job, especially if expansion of the company is progressing at a rapid pace.

It is better to begin the job with duties that will not fill the time allotted than to overload a new employee. This will result in high turnover. Other duties may be added to a new job as the person becomes acclimated. The illustration at the left provides an example of what the completed form may look like.

III. Writing Job Descriptions

Based on the completed analysis, a job description can be written.

The Basics

The description should include the following components:

1. A brief overview of the position (2-3 sentences) describing its basic function and the role it plays within the rest of the organization.

2. A list of functions, as delineated in the job analysis.

3. An explanation of the reporting structure for the position. (To whom does the position report and who, if anyone, does the position supervise?)

   Describe how the new hire will be interacting with other employees and what the job means to the progress of the company. Understanding of these roles may very well be the deciding factor in whether your top candidate accepts the position offered.

4. Necessary qualifications required for the positions. One should be careful to identify only those requirements actually necessary, i.e., licenses, certifications, technical degrees, etc. Requiring "a college degree" does not reflect what is actually necessary and may be construed as discriminatory.

5. List possible sources of job satisfaction and dissatisfaction. Listing satisfiers and dissatisfiers and reviewing this list

---

Job Audit

Audit conducted by _John Jennings_ ___ Date _Sep. 3, 1993_ ___

Job title _Assistant Store Manager_ ___

Major duties:
- Open & close store including cash register
- Schedule employees
- Participate in design of store displays
- Serves as a salesperson 50% of time.
- Maintains inventory control.

Minor duties: Trains new employees in company policies & sales hires new employees as needed Constructs store displays

Is supervised by (state relation): Store Manager

Number of employees supervised (state relation): Supervises all employees in store. Has authority to hire new employees. Provides input to manager on discipline.

Training required: Primary training in supervision. Additional training in sales promotion.

Education required: High school graduate. College coursework helpful especially if in business administration.

Certificates/licenses required: Valid driver's license.

Experience required (identify specific skills): Previous mgmt experience preferred. Ability to operate an NCR cash register. Open & close a cash drawer.

Physical requirements: Must be able to lift 50 lbs. Corrected vision to 20/100

On-the-job hazards/working conditions: Must lift & move inventory and furniture correctly to avoid risk of back injury.

Source of job audit information: Interviews with 2 assistant managers and 1 other store manager. Research with neighboring stores in mall.

---

prior to interviewing candidates, will help you to better evaluate candidates' suitability for the position.

6. Training necessary. This might involve specific training on a piece of equipment, a particular procedure, or set of standards. Having this information in the description insures an accurate assessment of what will be needed before the new person can become productive.

7. How performance will be appraised. Include specific measurements and accomplishments.

8. Specify what job opportunities would probably become available to the holder of this job should it be performed well. This will help you weed out the candidates who are not really suited to the organization's growth needs.

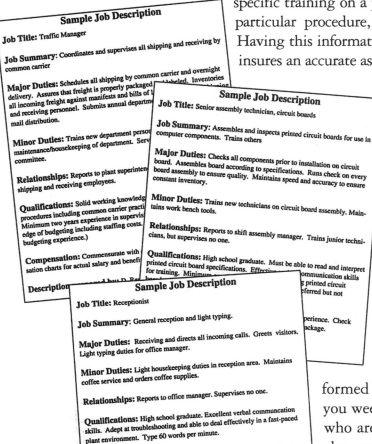

Sample Job Description

Job Title: Traffic Manager

Job Summary: Coordinates and supervises all shipping and receiving by common carrier

Major Duties: Schedules all shipping by common carrier and overnight delivery. Assures that freight is properly packaged and labeled. Inventories all incoming freight against manifests and bills of lading. Trains shipping and receiving personnel. Submits annual department budget. Oversees mail distribution.

Minor Duties: Trains new department personnel. Oversees maintenance/housekeeping of department. Serves on safety committee.

Relationships: Reports to plant superintendent. Supervises shipping and receiving employees.

Qualifications: Solid working knowledge of shipping and receiving procedures including common carrier practices and regulations. Minimum two years experience in supervision required. Working knowledge of budgeting including staffing costs. (May substitute college for budgeting experience.)

Compensation: Commensurate with experience. See compensation charts for actual salary and benefits.

Description prepared by: D. Resnick

Sample Job Description

Job Title: Senior assembly technician, circuit boards

Job Summary: Assembles and inspects printed circuit boards for use in computer components. Trains others

Major Duties: Checks all components prior to installation on circuit board. Assembles board according to specifications. Runs check on every board assembly to ensure quality. Maintains speed and accuracy to ensure constant inventory.

Minor Duties: Trains new technicians on circuit board assembly. Maintains work bench tools.

Relationships: Reports to shift assembly manager. Trains junior technicians, but supervises no one.

Qualifications: High school graduate. Must be able to read and interpret printed circuit board specifications. Effective as a trainer for training. Minimum ... communication skills ... printed circuit ... preferred but not ... experience. Check ... package.

Sample Job Description

Job Title: Receptionist

Job Summary: General reception and light typing.

Major Duties: Receiving and directs all incoming calls. Greets visitors. Light typing duties for office manager.

Minor Duties: Light housekeeping duties in reception area. Maintains coffee service and orders coffee supplies.

Relationships: Reports to office manager. Supervises no one.

Qualifications: High school graduate. Excellent verbal communcation skills. Adept at troubleshooting and able to deal effectively in a fast-paced plant environment. Type 60 words per minute.

Compensation: Hourly wage commensurate with experience. Check current compensation chart for actual wage and benefit package.

Description prepared by: D. Resnick

There are a host of software programs available to assist you in developing job descriptions.

Additional Considerations

In addition to the above, consider these points:

- All titles and language should be non-sexist.
- The descriptions should be about the job, not about the present job holder.

- Factors included should outline in detail what needs to be done, not what is being done presently. In some cases, the present job holder may be doing more or less than necessary.
- Be careful of including artificial requirements. The person in the job may have a college degree, but is one necessary to perform the job?
- Take care not to include discriminatory requirements (age, sex, physical characteristics, education, etc.). If you think it *might* be discriminatory, it probably *is* discriminatory.

After the description has been written, it should be reviewed for clarity, specificity, accuracy, and possible discriminatory requirements. These descriptions should be reviewed on a periodic basis to insure their accuracy. This saves valuable time when hiring.

Compensation should not be listed on job descriptions since it changes frequently and that would necessitate constant updating of the descriptions themselves. A salary and compensation schedule can be established for all positions. This practice also helps maintain consistency between individuals holding the same and comparable jobs.

IV. Determining Compensation

Before setting compensation for any position, its best to develop a *compensation philosophy*. For example, a company may decide to pay less and be a "training ground" for other larger companies in the area; or they may decide they want to beat the competition by paying a percentage higher than the going rate. While the first will result in increased training costs, the latter will increase compensation values. Before defining your salary schedules, step back and consider your philosophy.

Factors to Consider

In developing a compensation strategy, you must also research several areas. These are:

1. compensation ranges within the industry
2. cost of living factors in the local community

3. supply and demand for labor
4. alternatives to traditional compensation

Compensation Ranges within the Industry

Every industry conducts periodic compensation studies. Traditionally, the professional associations connected to an industry are responsible for this information. If the field is unionized, these organizations will also serve as a reliable source for such statistics.

Cost of Living in the Community

The cost of living within the local community will need to be taken into consideration. Some communities vary as much as 10% from those ten miles away. The chamber of commerce and government offices will be able to provide up-to-date information.

Compensation Profile
Comparison of Coverage

Position_____ Date Surveyed_____

Source of survey data:_____

Type of Compensation	Present Company Policy	Competitor's Policy	How we Compare	Plans and Recommendations
Wages				
Salary increase				
Bonuses				
Profit sharing				
Flexible hours				
Paid vacations				
Paid holidays				
Paid sick leave				
Paid disability				
Other leaves Jury duty Funeral Military Marriage Pregnancy				
Health insur.				
Dental insur.				
Disability ins.				
Life insurance				
Pension plan				
Savings plan				
Credit union				
Education ben.				
Children's ben.				
Other				
Other				

Supply and Demand for Labor

Research the labor pool for the various positions you normally fill within your organization. Once again, the chamber of commerce, state department of labor and the local job service will be able to provide estimates. You might also try local chapters of trade associations. Compare this information while looking for consistency. Compare notes with colleagues in like situations.

Alternatives to Traditional Compensation

There is a wide range of alternatives that should be considered when calculating compensation. Perks such as memberships, special equipment and subscriptions should be examined for their tax benefits.

Factors affecting working conditions such as flex-time and additional staff support, especially at the upper levels are sometimes most welcome. In addition, day-care centers, athletic facilities, on-site cafeterias, and other such services contribute to the feeling of being well compensated and may not be as expensive as straight salary.

More and more firms are turning to cafeteria style benefit programs where each employee chooses benefits according to need. Some companies give each employee a certain amount to spend on benefits per year with the unused portion going directly into the employee's pocket. In this way, single individuals are not paying for benefits they don't need. Investigate these options. They are becoming increasingly popular.

Incentives can also play a role at all levels of an organization. Rather than granting raises, more organizations are giving bonuses, prizes, and non-salary incentives to improve productivity. You might, for example, provide deep discounted trips for two to a nearby resort or present the "employee of the month" with six months of gasoline. Examine the possibilities of this area thoroughly.

Assembling the Information

Once the research has been assembled, the compensation for each type of position will have to be calculated. While the considerations for top levels may vary from production or line personnel, all factors need to be considered.

With a senior-level position, for instance, one might include more alternative forms of compensation such as travel expenses, professional memberships, and profit sharing. While production compensation may be based on more straight salary, perhaps a say in working conditions and incentives might be included. In all cases however, every factor must be weighed and considered.

Sample Hourly Wage Rate Table

COLORADO DIVISION OF EMPLOYMENT AND TRAINING
JOB BANK   JULY 1985 -   JUNE 1986
STATE OF COLORADO
TABLE V

HOURLY WAGE RATES FOR SELECTED OCCUPATIONS

OCCUPATION CODE	EMPLOYER JOB TITLES	JOB OPENINGS RECEIVED PAY SCALE		
		MINIMUM	AVERAGE	MAXIMUM
313381010	BAKER (HOTEL & REST)	3.35	5.06	7.25
313671010	SHORT ORDER COOK II	3.35	4.05	5.00
313684010	BAKER HELPER (HOTEL & REST)	4.50	4.75	5.00
315361010	MESS COOK	2.31	4.43	7.62
316684018	MEAT CUTTER	3.50	5.28	8.00
317684014	PANTRY-GOODS MAKER	3.35	4.32	5.75
317684018	SANDWICH MAKER	3.35	3.73	5.25
317687010	COOK HELPER	3.25	3.76	6.85
318687010	KITCHEN HELPER	2.40	3.74	7.50
319137010	FOOD-SERVICE SUPERVISOR	3.45	4.97	6.00
319474010	FOUNTAIN SERVER	2.50	3.74	5.50
320137014	LODGING-FACILITIES MANAGER	2.08	4.71	7.70
321137010	HOUSEKEEPER	2.50	2.75	6.38
323687010	HOSPITAL CLEANER	2.00	4.41	7.00
323687014	HOUSEKEEPING CLEANER	1.92	3.91	7.50
332271010	COSMETOLOGIST	3.35	3.81	5.00
352667010	RECEPTIONIST	3.35	4.20	5.50
354374010	PRACTICAL NURSE	2.03	5.30	6.50
355377014	PSYCHIATRIC AIDE	3.50	5.44	7.50
355674010	CHILD-CARE SCHOOL ATTENDANT	3.35	3.44	4.35
355674014	NURSE AIDE	2.03	3.78	8.00
355674018	ORDERLY	3.35	4.22	6.19
355677010	HOSPITAL-FOOD-SERVICE WORKER	3.35	3.60	4.14
359677010	CHILDREN'S INSTITUTION ATTDNT	2.00	4.08	7.50
361665010	MACHINE WASHER (LAUND)	3.35	4.19	5.00
361685018	LAUNDRY WORKER II	3.35	4.16	6.00
361687014	CLASSIFIER (LAUND)	3.90	3.90	3.90
361687018	LAUNDRY LABORER	3.35	3.68	6.38
363682018	MACHINE PRESSER	2.75	3.69	5.00
363684018	HAND PRESSER	3.35	3.90	5.00
372667018	CORRECTION OFFICER	3.35	5.45	6.50
372667022	TRAFFIC-CONTROL FLAGGER	3.35	5.69	7.91
372667034	SECURITY GUARD	2.52	4.61	7.25
372667038	MERCHANT PATROLLER	2.31	4.37	8.00
373364010	FIRE FIGHTER	2.86	6.84	7.50
375263014	POLICE OFFICER I	5.50	6.16	6.92
381137010	JANITORIAL-SERVICES SUPERVISOR	2.75	5.08	6.90
381687014	COMMERICAL OR INSTL CLEANER	3.35	4.04	7.23
381687018	INDUSTRIAL CLEANER	3.35	4.65	7.75
382664010	JANITOR	2.50	4.18	7.84
389684010	EXTERMINATOR	6.00	6.00	6.00
401683010	GRAIN FARMWORKER I	4.00	5.04	6.92
402687010	VEGETABLE FARMWORKER II	3.35	3.52	4.00

Sales Compensation

While sales drive any company, it is difficult to calculate a balance in compensation that is both equitable and attractive. Sales people are motivated by various factors. However you pay, it must be satisfying and yet must provide incentive.

One company set sales compensation for a new product at a particular rate. It was soon discovered that a hard-working salesperson could earn more in nine months than the vice-president would earn in one year. When commissions were cut however, the company promptly lost three quarters of its sales force.

This scenario is not uncommon. But it's difficult to pinpoint a level of compensation that is both attractive and yet retains some incentive for a sales person to work harder.

When developing a sales compensation plan consider the following:

- Examine the motivations of individual salespeople. What incentives have they responded to in the past? Ask them what they would find most attractive as compensation. Individuals are motivated differently.

  If you are hiring new sales people ask them about compensation at their last job. How were they paid? What kind of incentives did they receive? Why did they leave? Was it due to compensation? Their responses will help you discover their motivations.

- Research your competitors. How do they compensate? Are there established industry standards? Have you checked industry trade studies? No matter what you are selling, someone else, somewhere is selling the same thing or something close. Find out who that is and what they're paying.

- Consider all options available. Once again, motivations differ. Be creative with your incentives. Make the earning fun and exciting. Trips to Tahiti are more interesting than an additional $2000 per year and the trip won't cost you as much. Besides, the scuttlebutt about the trip will go on for years.

Increased benefits, perks around the office, better job titles, even the possibility of equity are all options to examine.

The *best policy* for organizing a sales compensation plan is to start with a small base and commission representing the lower end of industry standards. You can always increase commissions, add incentives, and give big bonuses.

You can never retreat from a compensation plan that pays too much. Regardless of reasoning, a reduction in commissions will be perceived as a cut in pay.

Compensation Policy

Developing a compensation policy for a large company can be a difficult task. But for most small- and medium-sized concerns, development of this policy is fairly easy. The policy should be straightforward and updated on a periodic basis. As the organization grows, increasing attention must be paid to these considerations. It is assumed that when the organization grows to 100 employees, a personnel department will be created to address these concerns.

A sample compensation plan can be found in Appendix C. Notice that it is aimed at the employees of the company.

Two final hints:

- If you are filling a vacancy, do not base the new employee's compensation on that of the former. For whatever reason, that salary may have been higher or lower. How you pay should be based on the merits of this new individual.
- Assume that everyone's compensation will be public knowledge. While you may wish to keep this confidential, it's impossible to do. The rumor mill will always discover hidden inequities in salary. Be prepared to justify them to anyone who asks.

V. A Checklist for Job Descriptions and Compensation

____1. Have you developed written job descriptions for all positions within your organization? (If yes, skip to question #4)

___2. Have you developed a checklist for determining whether a new position is needed?

___3. Have you developed a quick and efficient system for auditing positions within your organization?

___4. Have you developed a formalized compensation plan including all positions within the organization?

___5. Does all compensation within the organization reflect accurate pay rates throughout your industry and community?

___6. Are all forms, titles, job descriptions and compensation policies written in a non-discriminatory way?

Chapter 4

Recruiting the Best

"I can't believe we've only received three applications for these positions,"
he said. "Does this mean we have to hire everyone that walks in the door? We
may get some real dorks!"

"I don't see how we have any choice," she responded. "Maybe you can shift
some of the more experienced people around and give these new people the easy
jobs. The new production run starts tomorrow."

"In Indianapolis, we'd unlock the door and they'd come rushing in," he
said. "I just don't get it."

Here's What You'll Learn

Finding the right person for the job is a complicated process. It can be hounded by impatience, favoritism, inadequate training in employee selection, poor labor pools, and a host of other barriers.

I. Recruiting as a Hiring Tool

As organizations continue to monitor costs more closely, each employee recruited becomes more critical. While so-called "bad hires" may have gone unnoticed in the past, the same person now stands out due to the increased burden on every employee. It has been estimated that a position with a $30,000 annual salary over ten year ultimately costs the organization $480,000 including recruiting costs, health benefits, and cost of living increases. Everyone knows who is making a contribution. The quality of the hire is also a reflection on the person making the decision.

The way you approach the process is very important. Traditionally, we have looked at recruiting through the organization and procedures surrounding it. While there are anti-discriminatory guidelines to be followed, the remainder of the process can be conducted in any way you wish.

All too often we rely on the standard list of questions or commercially-bought application blanks to determine what information we should seek. Unfortunately, these tend to be shallow and generic.

Instead, someone in the position to hire should be identifying what is important to them. Many times we hesitate to dig deep enough into what we want for fear of not being able to find a person who fits the entire bill. The chances are good that you never will. But it is better to aim for perfection than to settle for mediocrity. As long as it's job related, you can ask any question you wish. So get specific in your expectations. Turnover or low productivity are expensive prices to pay for not defining your needs up front.

Remember that candidates are screening you as much as you are screening them. Employees are much more concerned about their ability to control their environment within the work place than they have been in the past. If your employees feel unable to control their surroundings, the growing scarcity of workers will allow them to simply vote with their feet and move to another employer.

A key ingredient for effective recruiting is being able to offer better work environments coupled with flexible benefits and generous training opportunities. Companies able to effect these changes become flexible work sites and have become the most successful employers in the 1990's.

Determining Needs

Consider the following ideas when developing your list of needs:

1. Consult the job description for the position. In addition to identifying actual duties, look for other attributes that might be helpful.
2. Determine the characteristics of your organization's culture. What attributes might a person need to fit in?
3. Who will be supervising the position? What attributes should a person possess to serve as a complement to this boss?
4. With what other individuals will this person have day-to-day contact? Are there certain group characteristics that need to be taken into account?
5. Look around your environment. What other factors might have to be taken into consideration to assure a thorough assessment of position characteristics?

This type of procedure should be followed with every hire. While it can be more time consuming, it also tends to assure effective hiring, low turnover and higher productivity.

II. The Recruiting Plan

While there is no exact way to determine optimum strategies for recruiting, you should develop a plan prior to approaching applicant pools. Comparing the actual results with the original estimates will provide an approximate picture of your effectiveness.

Here are some considerations:

- What positions are you presently seeking to fill?
- Which of these jobs can benefit from the same advertising?

- Which of these jobs should not be advertised with others? (i.e. Don't cluster shop foremen with accountants.)
- What is the expected turnover? If you are expecting high turnover as in retail, your standards for acceptable applicants may be lower than for a long term professional.
- Who are your targeted applicant pools? Applicants for different positions will be recruited from different sources.
- What are the best strategies for approaching the pools selected?
- What staff resources will be necessary to complete this project?
- How far in advance will you have to recruit to fill upcoming vacancies? Develop a time line.
- What are the recruiting messages being used with different applicant pools? Try not to mix these strategies. It will confuse people.
- Does your plan include the recruiting of minorities and other protected classes?
- Are the strategies proposed consistent with your organization's image. Would you advertise for bank tellers for instance, on bumper stickers?
- What will the project cost? Be sure to include expenses such as staff time, postage and phone charges.
- What approvals are necessary for this project to begin? Be cognizant of building support among those who hold the necessary influence.

MEMORANDUM

TO: Alex Raski, Vice President

FROM: Janet Forthright, Human Resources

After surveying all departments, I have established the following recruiting plan. We will be using a few rather non-traditional techniques this time. Hopefully, they will improve our applicant base, especially for assembly technicians.

Note: The numbers next to each job title are the number of individuals we expect to hire this quarter.

1. Assembly technicians (32)
2. Quality control technicians (21)
3. Shipping clerks (9)
4. Customer support clerks (15)
5. Billing specialists (7)
6. Secretaries (7)
7. Assembly supervisors (6)

Recruiting Technique	1	2	3	4	5	6	7
Direct mail to selected customers	●	●					●
Newspapers	●	●	●	●	●	●	●
Employee referral campaign	●	●	●	●	●	●	●
Local JTPA program	●	●	●				
Signs on local transit	●	●		●		●	
Morning TV spots	●		●		●	●	
Posters at all 7 community colleges	●	●	●	●	●	●	●
Letters to churches and senior center		●			●	●	●

We are also considering an open house hosted by Jack "The Coach" Razoon of WPLG. He should draw a big crowd. Let me know what you think.

Alex, we really need to get a handle on this turnover problem. We can only go to the well so many times. It's costing us a fortune!

Recruiting Plan Options

Develop a functional chart to organize the actual process. Keeping an eye on the flow graphically will help you stay on top of the plan's implementation.

Plan Evaluation

Recruiting plans can be measured several different ways:

Cost per hire is determined by dividing the total expense of the plan by the number of hires. Be sure to include all indirect expenses such as clerical and planning time. Calculating cost per hire enables you to analyze your effectiveness in hiring quality candidates economically.

MEMORANDUM

TO: Alex Raski, Vice President

FROM: Janet Forthright, Human Resources

We have completed evaluating the results of our first quarter recruiting campaign. While we did not receive the number of applicants we would have preferred for certain positions, we did meet our targets.

Job Title	Hiring Target	Appli. Target	Appli. Response	Actual Hires	Best Method
Assembly technicians	32	120	69	30	Local JTPA program
Quality Control Sup.	21	100	42	21	Posters at comm. coll.
Shipping Clerks	9	30	27	8	Signs on local transit
Customer Supp. Clerks	15	70	61	15	Posters at comm. coll.
Billing Specialists	7	28	20	7	Newspapers
Secretaries	7	21	15	7	Letters to senior center
Assembly Supervisors	6	30	37	6	Posters at comm. coll.
TOTALS	97	399	271	94	

Comments: Morning TV spots did not work as planned. Most were aired before 7AM, against our wishes. The results did not justify the expense.

The open house was a tremendous success. The trouble is, we can't do it 4 times a year. It also played havoc with the Saturday shift.

The JTPA program worked fine. I was skeptical of the first five applicants, but they have a better attendance rate than everybody else. I think we have discovered something!

The new ideas such as transit signs and that balloon giveaway at the mall appear to be bettering our image. On to the next quarter!

Recruiting Plan Evaluation

Vacancy rates allow recruiters to evaluate the patterns of frequency in the turning of employees. It is calculated by dividing the number of open positions by the total number of positions when the organization is fully staffed. This information can be instrumental in discovering escalating turn-over among certain jobs.

Selection rates enable you to see the ratio between the number of people interviewed and the number hired. This information is obtained by dividing the number of interviews by the number of hires. Selection rates help you to determine the quality of the candidates being interviewed. If your selection rate is low, your pre-interview screening techniques may need to be evaluated.

Referral rates illustrate the return on recruiting advertisements. A low return means that the effectiveness of the ad needs to be improved. Referral rates are calculated by dividing the number of people who responded to the ad by the number of those who were actually qualified for the position. If, for example, you receive 200 responses to a particular campaign and only 25 are qualified, the targeting of the ad probably needs adjustment.

Recruiting plans, if carefully developed, can be extremely valuable in conducting a quality and cost-efficient recruiting campaign. In addition, plans such as this insure your compliance with equal opportunity and affirmative action requirements.

III. Budgeting for Recruiting

Recruitment of employees can be an expensive process. Most surveys published on hiring indicate the average professional hire costs approximately $5000. Studies covering the trades and unskilled labor indicate averages around $700.

With labor shortages, it becomes even more important to monitor the recruiting budget closely. It is easy for instance, to over-spend in a particular area simply because there is a sudden need for labor. A little planning will reduce the number of times this happens. This in turn, will help keep the recruiting budget within limits.

There are, of course the expenses of training, along with the occasional executive hire which will cost more. But, for the most part, recruiting expenses should be carefully watched.

Look for innovative, inexpensive ways to get the recruiting word out. Participating in or sponsoring local school events

---

Memorandum

To: Alex Raski, Vice President

From: Doris Resnick, Administrative Manager

Here are the comparisons between hiring the new customer service manager and the customer service receptionist we just replaced

	Manager	Receptionist
Cash Expenses		
Classified advertising	$500	$100
Postage, phone, misc.(est.)	75	0
Labor & Management time		
Search planning meetings	415	0
Develop and place classified ads	35	15
Administration of search	350	0
Review of applications	70	15
Phone interviews	175	0
Interviews	420	75
Second interviews	280	30
Decision making	175	15
Negotiation	70	0
Orientation and planning	350	30
Training	1650	150
Secretarial support	120	27
Miscellaneous administration	175	15
GRAND TOTAL	$4860	$482

Note: These totals do not include the unproductive training time on the new hire's part.

---

for instance, can be a great way to garner attention for your company and attract teenage applicants. You might attempt trades of service or products with organizations who have the ability to promote your need for applicants. In both of these cases, the actual costs should be minimal.

What's Included

There are several areas require consideration including overhead, staff time, phone expenses and managerial time. The table on page 52 illustrates a typical method for hiring one professional and one receptionist. Your costs may vary slightly, depending on your location. Occasionally calculate your company's hiring costs to remind everyone of the substantial expense resulting from careless selection and improper training.

Saving Money

How can you save money in the recruiting process? Be practical and creative. Ask plenty of questions and approach the process with a common sense perspective.

Costs can be reduced significantly if more attention is paid to the overall investment of time and expenditures. In many organizations, the recruiting process is not mobilized until a position actually needs to be filled. If a supervisor is hired in January for instance, it's quite possible that those hiring for the same type of position three months hence will begin a new campaign to collect applicants for the current opening. A one hour investment in calling those candidates involved in the process last time, may reveal two or three pre-screened individuals who are still interested.

A policy of "we are always looking for good people," even though there may be no openings at the time can save back-breaking work when someone is needed in a hurry. Encouraging employees to be on the lookout for possible applicants not only builds candidate pools, but investment in the organization. Besides, it doesn't cost a thing!

It is best to start from the beginning when developing recruiting procedures. Examine every step and ask, "How can I save money and still accomplish this task effectively?" Here are a few hints to help you:

- Look to internal referrals first, whenever possible. This could save the majority of recruiting costs. (See part IV in this chapter.)
- Concentrate on local hiring. There is no reason to pursue out-of-state candidates, if someone suitable can be found in your own backyard.
- Be extremely judicious in the use of headhunters and employment agencies. You are not necessarily saving money or getting the better candidate. Check references and reputation before proceeding. (More about this later in the chapter.)
- Keep a constant eye on costs. Remind those doing the hiring that recruiting is a cost center. Cut corners when you can.

IV. Internal Recruiting and Referrals

Recruiting from within or using referrals are the most cost effective ways to fill vacancies. While there can be drawbacks, these strategies offer several benefits.

If promoting from within, the employee already knows the organization and is a proven worker. In addition, overall employee morale will be improved since they realize that it is possible to advance within the organization.

Personal referrals from employees or outsiders provide information of a more personal nature on an applicant. They also provide the reputation of the person referring, and the saving of valuable recruiting dollars.

The drawbacks of using these strategies can be a limitation in your choice of candidates. There is the potential for rancor within the company if intentions are not totally clear. There may be understandable disappointment if the insider or referral is not selected. It is also difficult to discharge someone who was recruited for the position from inside the company if that person doesn't work out.

Defining the Plan of Action

In order to conduct an effective and fair selection process by either of these methods, you must have a defined plan of action. Consider the following:

- Assure clear communication about openings within the organization. Make sure that everyone knows what's going on. This eliminates rumors, misinformation and hard feelings.
- Develop a workable system. Posting a position for five days for instance, does not allow enough time for people to think about it. Be sure there are no hidden barriers. Standards that are too high or too specific can be disheartening as well as discriminatory.
- When you are considering a person in a certain department, make sure that the supervisor is aware of your interest. Marching in and "stealing" someone, even though it may be a promotion, will create animosity.
- Be open to new ideas in referrals. When we start looking for likely candidates, we tend to have a picture in our heads about what we would like. When something unusual comes up, we tend to ignore it. Test out new ideas. Consider individuals who did not become apparent right away. You may be pleasantly surprised.
- Keep a record of referrals and the people who made them. If the referral worked out, you may want to go to that person again for help. If it didn't, you may want to avoid referrals from that person. Be sensitive however, to the possibility that an unequal amount of impact may result from these lists if the referrals are coming primarily from a small group of employees.
- Provide incentives for referrals. Incentives could include a bonus, time off, a prize, plaque, or something else; these types of carrots can get everyone looking for good applicants.
- Remember to make sure that you clearly state what type of person you're seeking. Otherwise you may be swamped with unsuitable candidates.
- Consider how much encouragement you and the executive level give to employees about moving up. If staff

sees that management is encouraging the possibilities of promotion, they will be more interested in applying for the vacancies.

- Set goals for hiring internally. This will demonstrate to employees that you really mean it. While there is a chance of becoming an inbred company, this possibility is slight. Ten to 20 percent of your annual hires should be in-house. Otherwise, turnover will increase because employees decide that there is nowhere to go within the organization.

V. Identifying Applicants' Motivations

Before developing any strategy for approaching applicants, it is important to examine the motivation of those you want to attract. This can be accomplished in several ways.

The most basic strategy is to simply list those attitudes likely to appear in your target audience. If you have the same experience, age, and background, you should be able to develop an accurate profile of recruiting materials and approaches.

In many cases however, those doing the recruiting and those being recruited vary significantly in age, values and experience. While you may have passed age eighteen, that does not mean you can identify with the attitudes of today's teenager. A more accurate means for getting necessary information is to ask the teenagers already working for you. This not only provides useful input, but also involves them in the process. Their ensuing interest may result in more enthusiasm for the job and even referrals of qualified applicants.

What to Ask
When surveying your applicant pools

Ask each individual these questions:

1. What is the most important feature to you in a job?
2. What was your last job? (*If employed, where are you working now?*)
3. Why did you accept that job?
4. What did you like best about the last job you held?
5. What did you like least about the last job you held?
6. Please rank the following from most important to least:
    a. Distance from work
    b. Hours
    c. Job duties
    d. Pay
    e. Work environment
7. What is the most important feature you look for in a supervisor?
8. How did you find out about your last job?

A final method is actually surveying those in your target group. This means getting on the phone and asking them what they want out of a job opportunity. While this can be time consuming and expensive, it may result in some good referrals *and* good information. Going directly to the market will also help enhance your organization's image.

VI. Enhancing Organizational Image

Before implementing a recruiting program, you should examine how your organization is perceived by the community. It is difficult to attract applicants when those in the targeted groups are not aware the company exists. It is even more difficult when they have a negative perception of what it is like to work for your organization.

You might conduct an informal survey to discover how those in the community feel. Explain to individuals what you're doing and ask broad, open-ended questions:

"What have you heard about our organization?"

"Do you use our products? What do you think of them?"

"Do you know people who work there? Do they like it?"

These surveys will provide information on what's being said, both positive and negative. While much of this is probably based on rumors and gossip, you still need to address those concerns that are having a bad influence on organizational image.

This type of information will also reveal other concerns that can be used in the recruiting process to attract candidates. These include attitudes about working conditions, hours, compensation and the like.

There are several areas to monitor when assessing and enhancing an organization's image:

Overall company public relations: Consult with those responsible for public relations. Provide them with information on new endeavors such as training programs, recruiting outreaches to special groups and affiliations with local schools. These all demonstrate the organization's citizenship in the community.

The media can have a tremendous impact on an organization's image. It is best to maintain good relations with them at all times.

Recruiting literature: Take a close look at the literature being used for recruiting. Does it accurately represent what the company does? Is it written for the prospective employee? Does it discuss working conditions, expectations and opportunities? Even for the most menial positions, a powerfully written brochure will make applicants want to work for you.

Recruiting signs and posters: The first impression you make on applicants may well be your last, unless they find your sign appealing. That appeal begins with design, type style, color, placement, instructions for applying and the work values it projects. Let's discuss each one of these elements and it's impact.

Applicant value messages: The words, "help wanted" have lost their effectiveness for attracting applicants. Everyone knows that you're looking for people. The posters that set you apart are the ones that appeal to values.

Recruiting Brochures

Just as brochures are necessary to sell your products, it is imperative that you have brochures and support material to assist applicants in understanding the value of your organization and why they should work for you. These brochures should speak to the applicants' concerns. The applicant is not the only person involved in their application. They consult with family and friends before making a decision. Those individuals will ask them about the job. The applicant's ability to answer those questions and, in the end, feel like they are making the right choice has a tremendous bearing on whether they will accept the position.

Designing the brochure:

- Begin by listing the possible questions and need the typical applicant will have. These items will probably include, a brief company history, it's role in the industry, the products you provide, image in the community, and organizational structure. Collect as many corporate recruiting brochures as possible and look for ideas that relate to your organization.

- Ask current applicants to make a list of what they would like to know about the organization and incorporate these thoughts in the brochure. Be sure to comment on the work environment and reporting structures within the firm. If there is one thing an applicant wants to know, is what it is like to work in the company.

- Prepare the brochure for easy reference. Lay it out so that different concerns can be located quickly and be shown to other individuals. Address the text candidates and write it in easy-to-understand terms. Use photographs to communicate the job content. Action pictures of the work environment and the people tend to lend credibility to the idea of working for you.

- Include quality of life information. Help applicants to understand that your firm has the employees best interests at heart. Stress opportunities for personal and professional growth, extracurricular activities and contribution to the company. Include evidence of long-term career potential. Provide employee testimonials and third-party endorsements that give candidates the idea that employees who work there enjoy what they do. Aim these remarks at candidates for the front-line positions since that is where you experience the greatest turnover.

- Summarize basic business facts about the company. Help candidates to understand the company's position within it's industry along with it's strengths and future. Recognize the changes in today's employees. Create a forward looking brochure that helps candidates see that your's is a forward looking company with potential for the future.

Each applicant has to be attracted the right way. But the "right" way depends upon *the applicant's* perspective. Every person has a different set of values and experiences. Senior citizens will not respond to offers of career advancement any more than teenagers will respond to health benefits.

Design: Just as we take time to carefully design product promotions, the same must be done for recruiting fliers. With the bombardment of information we now see in stores, a recruiting poster will only get a second's glance. If the information is not easy to understand, the reader will move on immediately.

Survey local employers prior to designing your own recruiting signs. What designs work and what don't? Why? Why are some easier to read than others? What phrases can you adapt to promote your message? Remember that the same sales techniques you use to sell products can be modified to attract applicants. The principles are identical.

Type style: It is easy to become fascinated with the variety of type styles available. But while you want to attract the reader with something interesting, be careful not to choose an unreadable face. A classic mistake in sign making is the use of a fancy type which, in reality, is too difficult to read at a glance. A second mistake is using more than three type styles on the same poster. While this may fascinate the sign maker, it will confuse the reader. Keep the sign simple and direct with as few words as possible.

Color: Choice of color can have a major impact on readability. Red printed on black for instance will blend into the background. Too many colors will distract from the message. Harsh colors, while attracting attention, may repel the reader. Even black on white can be readable and inexpensive.

Placement: Where do the people you want to attract gather? At a store? In the community center? At the local school? The best way to find out is to ask. Check with the people who presently work for you.

Application instructions: "Apply within," just doesn't cut it. Where within? To whom within? Most job searchers are shy about asking questions in the first place. To make them play a guessing game will scare many away. Be friendly, but specific with your directions. Give the location, whom to ask for, and the hours applications can be completed. Always provide a person's name and title.

Recruiting approaches: Have you examined the strategies you are using to approach applicants? Are they tailored to address the values of the targeted populations. Advertising exciting advancement opportunities to retirees, for example, will not have the impact of offering flexible schedules.

Front-line reception of applicants: When applicants make contact, how are they treated? Is the phone answered courteously? Does the receptionist have the correct information? Are there individuals available to speak to the applicant? A positive first impression goes a long way toward selling the job.

Handling of the selection process: Is the process simple and straightforward? Are deadlines met? Are candidates handled professionally? Are interviewers prepared? Is an effort being made to "sell" to the top candidates?

Employee turnover: After employees have left an organization, they are bound to talk about their experiences. While there are some who will have been discharged, the vast majority will have left on their own. Their comments about long hours, difficult supervisors, lack of opportunity and so on, can seriously damage your organization's image. This is another good reason to work toward reducing turnover as much as possible.

The "Sales" Pitch

Everyone associated with the organization's hiring should be able to discuss this topic at a moment's notice. Some of the best candidates come through referrals and informal introductions. Managers able to take advantage of these situations by speaking intelligently about openings and opportunities will acquire some top performers.

The best approach for this is a "30 second commercial." Prepare what you would say in advance. Include information describing the company, its opportunities, and tailor the rest to what you think would attract the person in question.

You might mention tuition reimbursement to a college student for example, or research and development funding to a computer specialist. Constant attention to organizational image will help you land the best people.

VII. Exploring Sources of Labor

The major factor of change in recruiting has been the evolution of labor sources. For the past twenty years, employers have taken the ample supply of inexperienced labor for granted. Much of this supply has consisted of students and homemakers looking for part-time work.

But as the so-called baby boom has grown up and the number of career women has exploded, employers have found themselves shorthanded. Every industry is experiencing the crunch for applicants.

Now that these sources are in short supply, we need to pay more attention to groups who have received a prejudicial eye in the past. These include:

Senior workers (those 55 and over)
Displaced homemakers
Moonlighters
Career changers
The physically disabled
The mentally disabled
Ex-offenders
Economically disadvantaged
Immigrants

Senior Workers

The largest and most influential of these groups are senior workers. Where 20 years ago, most individuals retired at 65, many more are continuing in their jobs or taking early retirement to pursue a new endeavor.

According to a survey conducted by the American Association for Retired Persons, 48% of those who said they were retired indicated that they would consider employment if the right situation appeared. As our population matures, the influence this group will exert in the work force will be enormous.

While myths surround the capabilities of older workers, most employers are finding these individuals work just as hard and efficiently as their younger counterparts. Due to maturity and experience, they are able to adapt quickly to new responsibility, deal with crisis, and get along with co-workers. Their loyalty to the company also tends to exceed that of younger employees.

The myth that you have to pay an older worker more money has also been found to be untrue. While there are some who command a superior wage, many choose other forms of compensation such as more time off, flexible hours and health benefits. Some may choose to limit their hours and/or compensation to avoid losing government aid such as social security and medicare.

Concerns about older workers tend to revolve around their ability to adapt to technology, their flexibility, and a lack of aggressiveness. While some employers are also troubled about lost time due to illness, statistics show that older workers and younger workers lose about the same number of days. Retirees and older workers in general, may be just what your company needs to maintain a reliable and relatively inexpensive staff.

Accessing the Market

To recruit older workers, the message must be tailored to their way of thinking. Appealing to job qualities they value will attract attention. These include flexible hours, flexible benefits, autonomy, opportunity to meet new friends, and working with people their own age. You might also stress that you value their maturity and experience.

The mediums for reaching this group are varied:

- Advertising in banks and post offices on the first of the month
- Community or church publications
- Bargain newspapers found at grocery stores
- Bulletin boards in communities where there is a concentration of older individuals
- Using testimonials of older workers within your organization
- Posters with tear-off coupons in malls
- Advertising in newspaper sections that appeal to older individuals
- Local senior centers

There are also an increasing number of retiree pools to be found in cities around the United States. You cannot advertise for "older workers" since this is discriminatory. The best means for locating these individuals is through the local chapter of the American Association of Retired Persons (AARP) along with churches and civic organizations.

Many cities have Forty-Plus clubs to assist members in pursuing employment. The individuals within these groups have generally been laid off by other companies.

The Small Business Administration's Senior Corps of Retired Executives (SCORE) might also be able to assist. These individuals are generally retired from business having started their own company in the past. Not only do they meet with likely candidates every day, but they themselves might be interested in working on at least a contract basis.

Examine the possible sources in your local area and discover how senior workers might fit into your organization.

Displaced Homemakers

Displaced homemakers are those women re-entering the work force after a long period of separation or those who are forced to work due to hardship. In some cases, these individuals have substantial skills and expertise. In others, they are inexperienced and may be entering the work force for the first time.

Depending on organizational need, the individuals in this group may be able to fill valuable roles. In most cases, training will be necessary to teach new skills for both job duties and for coping with the balance between business and family.

The Displaced Homemakers Network (202-628-6767) provides nationwide assistance to these individuals for training and placement. In addition, local agencies such as the YWCA will be able to identify other organizations that provide assistance.

Moonlighters

While many employers have discouraged moonlighters in the past, this group offers a pool of part-time labor to fill a variety of jobs. The key to attracting these individuals is stressing flexibility in schedules. They can best be reached through advertising aimed at groups such as teachers, police officers, fire fighters, skilled trades workers, retail clerks, and other hourly employees. If you are especially interested in part-time workers, you might also try college students, homemakers and individuals who can only spare part of their day.

Job Sharing

An alternative to flexible schedules is job sharing. This allows two individuals to complete the job by arranging their schedules and, at the same time, assuring the employer of a full time worker. Individuals responsible for the care of children and/or elderly parents are especially attracted to this opportunity. While the individuals selected for this type of job must be chosen carefully, the investment of time and effort is likely to pay off since there are not many opportunities of this nature available.

Retired or Exiting Military

While employers look upon those leaving the military as an excellent source of skills and experience, many of these individuals find landing a civilian job somewhat difficult. Much of this is due to the adjustment into a civilian environment along with the challenge of translating skills into business terminology.

To attract these individuals, you have to approach them in ways with which they can identify. These include such things as testimonials from former military personnel who have joined your firm or by holding an open house for retiring military if you are located in an area with a high military concentration.

Advertisements should be written with slogans and terminology that will catch their eye. Phrases such as, "Join our team" or "We need your discipline," will attract that split second of attention you need to convince them to read on.

Put military applicants at ease and make them feel welcome when they contact you. Helping them to adjust to an unfamiliar environment will win them over. You might offer a free workshop to help them with job search in the civilian world. Include some information on opportunities within your organization and how they might fit in.

To reach exiting military personnel, you must advertise in areas they frequent and publications they read. You might for instance, distribute fliers in stores and housing complexes where there are concentrations of military personnel. A billboard outside a local base will also attract attention.

There are also a number of military publications distributed nationwide. These provide an excellent means for contacting these highly qualified individuals. Call an installation near you for more information.

Career Changers

Those contemplating a change in careers can be another good source of labor. The average person switches fields three to four times and these individuals may be tapped to fill roles in your organization.

While there are plenty of these people outside your organization, there may also be a number inside who are growing restless. Look for better ways to keep those already on board more satisfied with the firm. Cross-training, professional development and educational assistance will all help prevent the loss of key individuals.

One of the best means for attracting career changers is to advertise "little or no training necessary." Many of those contemplating a move may look upon this an opportunity to gain a foothold in their new area of interest.

Target your recruiting messages to those populations you feel will yield the largest number of respondents. These might include teachers, clerical positions, retail clerks and manual laborers. There are a number of individuals within these ranks with good skills who are looking for an opportunity to prove themselves.

Mediums for reaching these groups include direct mail, advertisement in publications they read frequently and telemarketing.

Disabled Individuals

The most underused pool of labor in the United States are working-age disabled adults. Even with enforcement of the Americans with Disabilities Act, many will still find it difficult to secure employment. Even if you want to employ them, the disabled, in many cases, are difficult to locate. Here are some resources:

State agencies: There are 84 state rehabilitation agencies throughout the nation. These organizations provide training to the disabled and help with placement into jobs. In some cases, job coaches are available to assist in the first few weeks of employment. A coach stands side-by-side with a severely disabled worker and helps that individual adjust to the job.

Most services of these agencies are offered free of charge along with training and equipment to make reasonable accommodation. (Contact the Job Accommodation Network, call 1-800-JAN-7234 or the Council of State Administrators of Vocational Rehabilitation, 1055 Thomas Jefferson St. N.W., Washington, D.C. 20007.)

Public-Private Partnerships

The Job Training Partnership Act (JTPA) provides training and placement assistance to disabled workers through local Private Industry Councils. These councils assess business needs in the community and identify training programs that can provide the necessary trained individuals. An arrangement is drawn up so that the firms needing workers hire those who meet their qualifications after they are trained according to the companies' parameters.

Projects With Industry (PWI) is sponsored by the U.S. Department of Education. Industry representatives identify those areas where the greatest job growth is anticipated and disabled individuals are trained to fill those positions. (Contact the U.S. Department of Education, 330 C St. S.W., Switzer Building, Washington, D.C. 20202)

Targeted Jobs Tax Credit (TJTC) is a tax incentive for employers who hire disabled workers. The program gives employers a credit against first-year's wages paid to the newly hired worker. (Check IRS publication 906)

Veteran's and Private Placement Programs

The Veterans Administration along with some private employment agencies assist with the placement of disabled individuals. The local Veterans Administration offices assist employers in locating physically or mentally rehabilitated veterans.

In addition, other organizations throughout the United States offer ways to employ disabled individuals. Check with local welfare agencies, colleges and rehabilitation facilities to locate these groups.

Ex-offenders

While the average employer may be hesitant about hiring ex-offenders, they are suited for a variety of situations. Although they have been convicted of a felony, they have also paid their debt to society.

But this branding tends to make their job search difficult. In hiring an ex-offender, you will probably obtain a grateful, and therefore hard-working and loyal employee.

In addition, the Targeted Jobs Tax Credit Act provides private employers with wage incentives during the employee's first year. Understandably, an individual of this nature should be carefully screened prior to making an offer.

Locating pools of these individuals can best be accomplished through state and local rehabilitation programs, job service offices and agencies within local justice departments. In many cases, these organizations provide job training in addition to placement services.

Economically Disadvantaged

A large, and mostly untapped, source of labor is what the government has defined as the "working poor." These individuals, on welfare programs such as Aid to Families with Dependent Children, choose not to work since they lose health care benefits when employed. If your organization provides benefits to its employees, these individuals may be an excellent source of labor.

While you may have some legitimate concerns about training, attendance and work ethic, most social services agencies test and train these individuals before they are placed in the market. In some cases, receipt of benefits is contingent upon the completion of certain programs. While an investment in job training and coping skills may be necessary up front, you will be rewarded by loyal employees.

Immigrants

With the advent of labor shortages, employers are beginning to look outside the United States for workers. Producers of high technology and the hospitality appear to leading this effort.

While heavily regulated by the Immigration and Naturalization Service, it is still possible to recruit individuals provided the company has an organized system for doing so, the proper legal support for immigration and a need of employers larger enough to justify the expense and effort.

Inside the United States, there are pockets of immigrants searching for work, but without the proper authorization. While it may be tempting to hire these individuals, the employers runs a significant risk and substantial fines.

What's in the Future

The future labor force will be significantly different than today. In addition to a new focus on the groups discussed above, more global considerations are on the horizon.

Traditionally, white, non-Hispanic males have been regarded as the prime group within the labor force because they tend to be more highly educated than minority men and more closely attached to the labor force than women. But according to the Bureau of Labor Statistics, this group will make up less than 10% of the 20 million people expected to be added to the labor force by the year 2000. This will reduce their share of the nation's total work force to less than forty percent.

So-called minority populations have begun to outnumber the majority in certain parts of the country. This is resulting in value changes along with the necessity of being bilingual.

As technology continues to absorb the menial jobs, workers will find knowledge-based positions the only ones available. Since it is becoming apparent that many younger workers lack basic skills and older workers lack computer skills, employers will be forced to assume a much greater role in employee training.

These are changes that are happening now and will continue into the next century. The organizations that adapt their recruiting to address these changes will be the ones that thrive.

VIII. Locating External Applicants

With changes in the work force, locating and attracting applicants has become increasingly difficult. As a result, employers are developing more innovative and aggressive strategies to reach sources of labor.

External applicants can be recruited through a variety of sources. These can be separated into six categories:

- Internet advertising and World Wide Web resources
- Recruitment advertising agencies
- Recruiting services
- College placement centers
- Public job services
- Newspaper advertising

Prior to considering these approaches, determine your criteria for the successful candidate. If a job description has been developed for the position, this is an easy first step.

Once you have determined the criteria, look back to other times when you have hired for that and similar positions. Determine where the successful candidates have come from. This should provide a solid picture of how to recruit for the present vacancy.

Available applicants come from different labor pools for different positions. Skilled labor, for instance, might best be located through classified advertising while executive level applicants normally come through referrals and headhunters. It is extremely important that you maintain up-to-date information on the labor pools in your area. Maintaining an informal list of possible applicants as you discover them can be helpful in an emergency when a vacancy needs to be filled immediately.

It is never a good idea to hire in a panic. But sometimes you are left with no other choice. This informal list and perhaps the collection of resumes and applications received in the past 90 days will ease the burden of screening all new candidates.

The abundance of applicants many companies are used to receiving has subsided. While this relieves the burden of paperwork, it also requires more diligence when recruiting. Applicants have to be convinced that working for your company can be a secure and rewarding experience. With the low unemployment in many states, applicants have to be lured and convinced that the best opportunity is with you.

Internet Advertising and World Wide Web Resources

The proliferation of the Internet and World Wide Web enables some employers to research labor markets and recruit applicants more efficiently that any system that preceded it. Simply input "resumes" into any one of the search engines and hundreds of entries for resumes and resume services will appear on the screen. Likewise, it is also possible to advertise positions quickly and affordably using the Web.

As with any resource, the key to using it effectively is having a plan. Here are some suggestions:

Determine if the applicants you seek use the Web. While much as been made about ensuring that every person will have access to the internet, the reality at this time is that a relatively small percentage of the work force can use it. Carefully research internet traffic before making a major commitment.

Make a list of key words associated with your industry and perform searches. Some people simply post their resumes in areas of the Web they think are most appropriate. They also hotlink (the words or phrases in blue) from other sites. As you search, you may also discover services that offer a collection of resumes specific to your industry. Be careful, however, to check references before doing business with them. You may be able to achieve the same results simply by posting positions at the right sites yourself.

Bookmark the sites that you find helpful. You might even program your computer to visit those sites once a week to review any additions or deletions.

Post your openings on the Web. If your organization has a Web site, that is the most obvious place to begin. But you might also post the positions on appropriate chat room bulletin boards. This can be specially help with technology positions.

Copy and save any information you would like to keep at the time you discover it. Some Web sites are notorious for going on- and off-line unpredictably.

Maintain adequate security on your system at all times.
Recruiting on-line can be unpredictable, at best. Look carefully before leaping.

Recruitment Advertising Agencies

Recruitment advertising agencies specialize in assisting organizations to attract qualified candidates. These companies offer expertise and creativity normally not available within your own organization. In addition, they concentrate on this area alone and therefore are more attuned to what strategies work. This is generally not an expensive service since the agencies receive their commission from the media in which they place ads.

Before proceeding with one of these organizations however, it is best to investigate what each one can do for you. You might ask the following:

- How large is the agency? Does it have multiple offices? If your organization has several sites, can any of these be used?
- What do other clients say about this agency? Ask for and check references.
- How much lead time does it need to prepare your campaign?
- What services are offered and which will be charged for? Some agencies offer extensive administrative services such as tracking advertising and results of campaigns. Will the company be charged for these extras? How much?
- How aggressive is the agency? In a tight labor market, more creative techniques must be used to attract candidates. Can this agency demonstrate a track record of innovative and unusual advertising that works?
- Does the agency demand a contract? If so, negotiate a trial period.

Recruiting Services

Results from working with services can range from fruitful to disastrous depending on the relationship you have developed.

Remember that these organizations are in the business to make money. Therefore, the faster a vacancy is filled, the more they profit. Unfortunately, the emphasis on speed can impair the quality of service. It is your responsibility as a client to define the parameters of the relationship and enforce quality control.

If, for instance, you have posted a managerial position, it is your responsibility to provide a definitive job description. In addition, you should list other critical qualities the successful applicant will have. This information enables the service to tailor its search and increase accuracy along with speed.

If however, the candidates being referred do not fit the position, turn them away. Agencies at times, will try to give the "hard sell" to a candidate they think is a match. Mistakes due to impatience, panic or even undue pressure can be costly at a later time.

These organizations may be separated into four categories: employment agencies, temporary agencies, executive recruiters and executive search firms (also called headhunters). Now let's examine the four recruiting service sources:

Employment agencies: These organizations generally serve as a clearinghouse for clerical and staff support positions. They can exact their fee from the employee, the client company, or both. A good agency can save you time and money by screening applicants and providing only those who are qualified. It is important however, to check the references of these organizations before you do business. The ones that have been in business the longest are usually the best. Review your budget before committing to these services. While it takes more time to do it yourself, those on a tight budget will save money.

These agencies are typically found in the local phone directory. However, you might ask colleagues for references too.

Temporary agencies: These organizations are different than employment agencies in that they pay the employee rather than the client company. Most enforce a monetary penalty on workers who accept a full-time position with a client. Increasing numbers of people are working on a temporary basis in this changing work force, so these agencies are enjoying a surge in popularity. These agencies can also be found in the phone directory, but it is best to get referrals.

Executive recruiters: These firms will assist you in hiring entry-level and mid-level managers. Their clients are primarily current job seekers. If you were to post your opening in the classifieds, you might come across many of the same names in the resulting stack of resumes.

Executive recruiters base their income on successful matches between company and applicant. They work on either a retainer or contingency basis. Many specialize in a particular industry and can be most helpful provided they have developed the expertise. Working with an effective executive recruiter can save valuable time in locating and screening likely applicants.

The cost of this service averages 30 percent of the new employee's first year salary. This can be an expensive option. Look closely before committing to this service.

Executive recruiters can be located through phone directories, the classified ads section of the local paper, business directories and referrals. The referral option is probably the best choice.

Professional/executive search firms (headhunters): The colloquial term refers to the fact that these individuals "headhunt" for corporate professionals or executives to fill senior positions in a client company. While the applicant finds the executive recruiter, the headhunter works exclusively for the company.

The process for this type of search is involved. The headhunter will begin by interviewing the company's management and fully investigating its organization. As with executive recruiters, these professionals usually specialize in one industry. Targeted professionals sought by headhunters are usually working managers in the field, who can be lured away to a more challenging and lucrative position.

The compensation for these services averages 30 percent of first year compensation. For most companies, the use of a headhunter should be strictly confined to filling senior-level positions. Interview these agencies carefully before securing their services. This should be done in your office. Ask for references from current and previous clients.

Another consideration regarding search firms is the concern that these same firms might lure away the same employees they had placed with you the year before. While most will refrain from recruiting these individuals for the first two years, it is still difficult to prevent them from approaching the same people thereafter.

In addition to recruiting services, there are other options available:

College Placement Centers

College placement centers offer a wealth of qualified candidates to fill many needs. Yet, it is primarily the larger companies that take the most advantage of what these centers have to offer.

Newly graduated students are an excellent source of state-of-the-art information. Student interns can work and learn in your company at the same time. While these individuals may take time to train, an internship also provides you with an excellent opportunity to determine whether they would make good full-time employees.

It is important to develop a relationship with colleges from whom you intend to recruit. Your presence on campus will have a positive impact on students and faculty, but only if it is nurtured.

Just as you would conduct an advertising campaign to attract applicants to production jobs, you must publicize your existence to students. This includes posters around campus, articles and advertisements in the school paper along with scheduling on-campus recruiting times with the placement office.

This nurturing process can also be accomplished by getting involved in campus activities. Sponsor events such as lectures, sports, and entertainment. Serve in the visiting executive program if there is one. Participate in job and career fairs.

Visiting with faculty and administrators is of primary importance. Many students rely on the advice of these professionals for guidance in deciding where to work. This is an especially helpful strategy in fields like engineering where demand for graduating students is high.

A college can also provide part-time help at less expense than the average employment agency. While these individuals must be paid, they are willing to work for less compensation in order to gain the practical experience and contacts. Call the placement office at your nearby college for additional information.

Public Job Services

There are a wide variety of public job services in your community who maintain lists of candidates from which to choose. Many times these organizations are unjustly maligned. Some are state and federally supported while others are sponsored by professional associations and civic groups.

The most effective strategy for locating the best applicants is to develop a relationship with the counselors or coordinators of these organizations. They will help you select individuals to address your needs.

Newspaper Advertising

Newspaper advertising is the most common means for announcing a vacancy. Unfortunately, it does not yield the desired results in many cases. The ad must be attractive and specific. Even then, there is a good chance of receiving a number of unwanted resumes.

With the tightening of labor pools across the United States, these brief ads don't have the effect they used to. What is put into a small space like this has to compete with hundreds of other openings.

Before advertising in the local papers, peruse the classifieds. Observe their layout and where the type of job you want to fill is placed. If your type of opening cannot be found easily, you should look for another medium. Most cities have two or three daily papers. Many times the so-called blue collar jobs are listed in one paper while white collar jobs are listed in the other. It tends to correlate with reader preference.

Besides the classifieds, you also have the option of placing a display ad. Much more can be done with a quarter, half or full page of a newspaper. The special effects unavailable in the classified ad can be used here to attract greater attention.

But advertising studies have shown that small space ads will draw 75-80 percent of the response of a full page for much less cost. While classifieds will not stand out as much as a display ad, it is probably wise to refrain from inserting more than a quarter page ad at any one time.

Avoid running four-line ads in major newspapers that are swallowed up by the ads surrounding it. Instead, place a display ad in a few local papers where your information will get more play. The extra space also allows for the opportunity to add work-life issues to the job description and qualifications.

Consider advertising in other areas of the paper besides the employment section. Some companies have had success attracting older individuals for instance, by placing ads in the obituaries.

Remember too, that most individuals search for employment near their homes. Advertising in the *New York Times* to recruit retail clerks for instance, is probably a waste of money since most of the newspaper's circulation will reach those outside the geographical area of interest.

In addition to local papers, there are regional and national publications that cater to a specific industry or profession. Unfortunately, these tend to be issued monthly or quarterly, and are not timely enough for the average opening. The one exception would be the large scale campaign to recruit a sizable number of employees. But this takes substantial advance planning.

IX. Creating an Attractive Job Notice

Writing a job notice is like writing an advertisement. The description must sell the job in the best light possible. At the same time, it must be honest and accurate. More than one company has lost a lawsuit over the wording in an ad that hid or exaggerated the true nature of a job.

Recognize that selling the position will also generate a number of unqualified applicants. If you have other positions to fill, this strategy might be a good way to collect resumes for those openings.

Follow these guidelines for writing the notice:

- Start the ad with an attractive and descriptive title. Be sure the title you use is an accurate representation of the job and something that those you want to attract will understand.
- Write a brief description of the duties. Be sure to include what makes this job attractive. Do not include the

obvious. Listing duties such as "development of software" in a job description for a computer programmer is redundant. Instead, include the uses of the software proposed and in what language. Providing information about the role of the position in the company helps to sell the job.

- List required experience and education.
- Ask for a salary history. This will help you screen candidates who may be applying over their head or for a position for which they are overqualified.
- Sell the benefits of the job. How will the applicant benefit by holding this position? What's unique? The first example to the left illustrates the value of selling benefits.
- Stress quality of work life issues with in the ad. Values such as ethics, reward for hard work, personal and professional growth are experiencing a resurgence of priority in candidates' minds.
- Avoid adjectives that do not demonstrate the job. "Exciting, challenging and rewarding, etc." are relative to the individual.
- Personalize the ad. Talking to the applicant instead of just listing duties and qualifications will make the reader stop and think. The first example on the next page attempts to convince the reader to apply. Notice the persuasive language in the job summary.
- Edit closely. Eliminate unnecessary words and phrases. Assume potential applicants will be able to follow the flow of the ad. Be careful however of abbreviations, however. These can be easily misunderstood or indecipherable.
- Answer the questions the candidate is most likely to ask. Put yourself in the reader's position. If you were reading the examples to the left as a job searcher, what questions would you have? Does this posting answer these questions? What would improve it?
- Listing salary is up to you. Some employers do not want their competitors to know how much they are paying. On the other hand, good candidates may not want to apply unless they know the nature of the compensation.

• The identity of the company can also be omitted at your discretion. Many large employers do this to reduce the number of unqualified applicants who are simply attracted to the name. Other employers do not provide their name because they do not want competitors to know they are hiring. Not listing the company name also releases you from having to respond to rejected candidates without losing good will in the job market. This can be advantageous when there is a large number of submissions.

WE'LL MISS YOU JACKIE

Jackie is our staff assistant and she's leaving. We're looking for someone to take her place. She can type 90 words a minute, (we'll take 65,) has flawless English skills and can handle our seven phone lines with ease.

If you think you can fill Jackie's shoes and would like to join a fast-paced, results-oriented company, call Susan Hobbs at 444-3987 right away!

Personalized Recruitment Ad

What's wrong with these ads?

CUSTODIAN - for a large apartment complex. Experienced and sober. Will be on call every fourth weekend. Knowledge of A/C and plumbing repair helpful. Apply in person: Forest Green Apartment Homes, 34 O'Toole Avenue, Markham, MA

SERVICE REPRESENTATIVE

To handle service calls for local distributor of electrical appliances. Will train. Reliable transportation a must. Mature man preferred. Call or apply in person: Health applicances, Inc. 344 Broad Street, Emerson, NJ 07665 456-6368.

WHAT A GREAT JOB!

ADMINISTRATIVE ASSISTANT to handle bookkeeping, reception and other duties. Permanent opening immediately available. Good writing and typing skills. Sense of humor. Able to work under pressure. Stable woman preferred. Apply to Mr. Storm, P.O. Box 3333, Lewiston, AL 98876.

KEY

#1 - May not use the word "sober" or imply abuse. "Every fourth weekend" you may have to make reasonable accomodation.

#2 - "Mature man" infers discrimination. "Reliable transportation." Employer is responsible for providing transportation or reimbursement.

#3 - "Stable woman" infers discrimination. Some courts have held that referring to a job as "permanent" means for the life of the employee.

Classified Advertising "The Right Way"

A WORLD CLASS COMPANY

DIGI-LECTRONICS is a fast growing subcontractor to the defense and computer industries. Our local plant is one of the most automated in the United States. We offer excellent benefits and training with an opportunity for advancement. We seek a:

LAB SUPERVISOR

Successful individual will supervise 8-10 technicians and must have experience in a printed circuit board environment combined with 3-5 years supervisory experience in a non-union environment. A degree in chemistry or chemical engineering required. We offer overtime and a 10% shift differential for 2nd and 3rd shifts. Send resume, letter of interest and salary history to: DIGI-LECTRICAL P.O. Box 13263, Fort Hassle, KY 77876

KITCHEN AND SERVICE PERSONNEL

We're looking for high energy individuals who enjoy challenges in a fast-paced environment to join our team. Experience is not necessary as we offer a complete training program. Apply in person between 2-4 pm weekdays to Cuisine Unique, 3404 S. Hempstead Blvd. Chicago, IL.

RETAIL MANAGER

National card, gift and sundry chain has an opening for store manager in a downtown location. No nights or Sundays. Two years of retail management experience or equivalent college training and customer service background preferred. Interested individuals should apply in person or call:

The Sundry Shop
2200 E. Kalamath Street
Littleton, CO
548-3759

On the other hand, good candidates may not apply simply because they fear the employer they are presently working for may be the advertiser. Some simply want to know where they are sending their credentials.

- How candidates may respond is up to you. For immediate hires such as staff and semi-skilled positions, it is best to have the applicants call for an appointment. In many cases, these individuals will not have resumes and will have to come down to complete an application.

If they do apply in person, be sure someone is available to spend a couple of minutes interviewing them. The public relations benefit of this is tremendous.

When you are hiring for a professional or executive position, ask for application by resume.

X. Developing Labor Pools for the Future

Organizations that thrive in the future will be pro-active in their development of consistent labor pools. This development must be implemented now and take place continually.

Here are a few key strategies for insuring your work force of the future:

- Recruiting awareness should become a way of life for all employees. This will insure a constant stream of referrals,—reward those who do refer.
- Maintaining positive employee relations is critical to the recruiting effort both inside and outside the organization.
- Continue to build corporate image at every opportunity. Maintain a constant flow of information about programs and special events taking place in the company.
- Anticipate changes in the community's demographics and therefore its labor force. Don't follow what the media is saying. Find out before they do!
- Closely monitor applications. Look for patterns in response from certain labor groups. This will provide keys to where you should concentrate your advertising.

- Maintain your aggressiveness in the pursuit of applicants. Be creative and try the unusual to attract attention.
- Hire the best when they appear. Even if you don't have an exact spot, do what you can to get them on board and take advantage of their enthusiasm and skills.
- Get rid of employees who don't produce. These individuals have a negative impact on the teamwork and energy of those who do. Consequently, applicants and new hires will develop the wrong impression of organizational culture.
- Know your organization's strategic plan and where you'll have openings in the next 12 months. Anticipation of need eliminates panic.

XI. A Checklist for Recruiting Basics

_____1. Have you developed a set of procedures and contingencies for recruiting within your company?

_____2. Have you included the cost of recruiting in your budget?

_____3. Have you developed a system for recruiting internally?

_____4. Have you developed a system for tracking referrals?

_____5. Do you provide an incentive program for referrals?

_____6. Have you developed a relationship with a reliable employment agency to serve your staffing needs?

_____7. Are you consistently checking your recruitment literature and advertisements for potentially discriminatory statements or inferences?

_____8. Once again, do you really need to fill the position? (See Chapter Three)

_____9. And again. Do you have a well-defined description for the job to be filled? (See Chapter Three)

_____ 10. Have you developed a profile for each of the applicant groups from which you recruit?

_____ 11. Have you begun to include senior workers in your recruiting plans for all levels of work?

_____ 12. Have you examined the feasibility of including disabled individuals in your staffing plans?

_____13. Have you examined the feasibility of including temporaries in your staffing plans?

_____14. Have you considered using contract managers and professionals in certain positions?

_____ 15. Have you developed a recruiting plan taking into consideration changes in your staffing needs and labor pools over the next five years?

_____ 16. Have you communicated the importance of recruiting and provided employees with the information necessary to "sell" the company?

_____ 17. Are you taking steps to get involved with local schools to foster relationships for recruiting students and graduates?

_____ 18. Do you regularly evaluate your organization's image?

_____ 19. Have you examined the variety of alternative work plans such as flexible scheduling and telecommuting for their suitability in your organization?

_____ 20. Have you organized and implemented an internship program with local schools?

_____21. Have you examined the way you are recruiting professionals to assure you are addressing their needs?

_____22. Have you developed an aggressive stance toward recruiting employees?

MOMS!

*Re-enter the work force and
still stay home with the kids!*

Fiesta Foods is always looking for individuals interested in working mid-day shifts as cashiers or clerks.

We offer:

Flexible hours

Competitive wages

Friendly atmosphere

Apply at any of our locations:
1017 S. Grant, Odessa
1613 W. County Road, Odessa

Get out of the house and into the store!

(for a job, that is)

Fiesta Foods is looking for talented individuals seeking to re-enter the work force on a part-time basis. Come grow with us!

We offer:
Flexible hours
Competitive wages
Friendly atmosphere

Apply at any of our locations:
1017 S. Grant, Odessa
1613 W. County Road, Odessa

NEED CASH? WORK HERE!

Fiesta Foods is looking for mature, reliable, individuals to work as:

Cashiers	Stock Clerks
Night stockers	Courtesy Clerks
Meat Clerks	Deli Clerks

Competitive wages
Flexible schedules
Practical Training
Management Training
Opportunity for advancement

Apply at any of our locations:
1017 S. Grant, Odessa
1613 W. County Road, Odessa

NOW HIRING SENIORS!

We're looking for mature, reliable individuals who enjoy a good day's pay for a good day's work. Come help us serve our customers with superior service by becoming a part-time clerk or cashier in this store.

We offer:
Flexible hours
Competitive wages
Friendly atmosphere
An opportunity to "un-retire"

It's easy to apply:
Just go to the customer service counter and ask for an application. We can get you started right away!

Sample display ads

Join Our Palm Tree Team!
Patty Sheenan did!

"Hi. I'm Patty Sheenan, a deli clerk here at the Alcorn Palm Tree Foods. When I started shopping here six years ago, I never dreamed I'd be working in this store. But when my kids started school, I decided to look for a part-time job, and there it was in my own back yard. We are truly a team here. The people are nice and the hours allow me to still be home when school lets out. Come see me in the deli and I'll tell you more about why this is such a great place to work."

Take after Patty and join our team!
If you'd like to know more about how to make extra cash and still be home with the kids, just come to the customer service counter in any of our stores and we'll get you started with an application.

Sample shopper insert

Chapter 5

Family & Friends: Dealing with Nepotism

The production manager was irritated. "I know he's your son and I know he's qualified," he said to the owner. "But I feel like I'm competing to keep my job. I can't use my discretion knowing that anything he questions is going to end up in your ear."

"Be patient with him," said the owner. "He's learning the ropes."

"Well let him learn someplace else," retorted the manager. "I'll be honest with you, Jack. If this continues, I'm going to start looking for a better situation."

Here's What You'll Learn

I.   Nepotism in Business
II.   The Pros and Cons of Family and Friends
III. The Legal Aspects of Nepotism
IV.   Devising a Nepotism Policy
V.   Tips on Screening Family and Friends
VI.   The Nepotism Checklist

I. Nepotism in Business

Hiring family and friends is a common practice in many companies. In fact, some of the nation's largest enterprises are family owned. At its inception, a company may consist of a spouse, two or three good friends and a couple of long-time business associates who believed in the idea.

The Small Business Administration has estimated there are 13 million family-owned businesses in the United States. These range in size from the nation's largest corporations to "mom and pop" companies that have been around for years.

Employers tend to rely more on referrals for their recruiting needs than any other source. It can be comforting to know that someone else you trust within the organization has known this individual and can attest to their character and work ethic.

Generally, a family member or friend has a larger psychological investment in the future of the organization. They know people in the firm and this makes it easier for them to adapt. They might work harder knowing whose livelihoods are depending on it.

II. The Pros and Cons of Family and Friends

There are a number of pros and cons to the hiring of family and friends. You must be careful to deal with these applicants the same way you would deal with an outsider. But while there can be unfortunate situations, there can also be substantial benefits.

Most research in the area of nepotism has revealed that even though it is prevalent throughout American business, there is not a lot of support for its practice. Below are some arguments for and against nepotism. You should decide for yourself whether this practice should be allowed.

Arguments for Nepotism

- Family members generally have a bigger psychological investment in you and the organization. If you started the company, they have probably heard you talk about it for a long time. It might feel as if the company is part of the family.
- Relatives of executives will feel a greater pressure to perform well because they are relatives. Where

non-relatives might "punch the clock," family members will try harder, due to the nature of the relationship.
- It takes less time to train and indoctrinate relatives.
- Relatives working together share common goals and values.
- Salespeople bearing the name of the company are more likely to impress clients.
- Family members and friends might be willing to forego a certain amount of compensation and throw in extra time knowing they will reap the rewards later.

Arguments against Nepotism

- Supervisors are intimidated by subordinates who are related to executives.
- Relatives who are not successful within the company are difficult to discipline or fire.
- Relatives tend to be pushed up the ladder within the company, preventing other more competent individuals from advancing.
- Employees are afraid of talking about business around relatives because they fear that these individuals are acting as spies.
- Related employees are frustrated because they are never sure whether they made it on their own or because of family influences.
- Family members can rarely meet the expectations of other employees.
- Many times, there is an assumption on the part of relatives or friends that they are a "shoe-in" for a job, simply because of their relationship with you or someone else within the company. If these people are not qualified for the job, it is not always easy to reject their application.

If they are qualified for the position, it may be very difficult to select someone else without insulting a number of friends or relatives. Further still, these applicants never quite know whether they were hired for competence or because they are members of the family. Other employees are never sure about this either, and this can cause some friction.

Termination of friends or relatives, if they do not work out, is difficult, if not impossible. You may be viewed as persecuting that individual, and creating a difficult situation within the entire family.

There are also issues of leadership transition. Will the son automatically follow in the father's footsteps? Does this practice send a message to the rest of the employees that there is little chance for advancement into the executive ranks?

Can these individuals be placed in sensitive positions, such as payroll, assistant to other executives, or areas where they would have access to confidential information about the future of the company? If you do not do this, is this a form of discrimination?

Finally, the hiring of relatives and friends has an influence on the morale of other employees. Questions of favoritism come into play. While these issues may not surface, assume they are being noted and discussed throughout the company.

III. The Legal Aspects of Nepotism

In addition to issues revolving around personal relationships, you must be cognizant of the legal implications of recruiting with regard to anti-discrimination legislation. While it is permissible to hire anyone you wish, the company must also meet equal employment/affirmative action standards if you have fifteen or more employees.

The practice of hiring on referral must be watched carefully to assure proper hiring procedures. Family and friends should be hired in the same manner as any other applicant. Consistency is a key factor.

A number of states have also passed legislation prohibiting discrimination on the basis of nepotism. This means that spouses cannot be denied employment because they are married to someone in the company. You may still prohibit that person however, from working under the direct supervision of a spouse or other relative.

In asking about possible relations within the organization, be aware of possible discriminatory practices. It is perfectly acceptable, for example, to ask if the applicant has relatives working for the company. However, selection decisions should not be based on this information.

Nepotism should not officially be encouraged. A statement in the nepotism policy or elsewhere that encourages the hiring of family and friends could be seen as having an adverse impact.

An example of this would be a firm that has a predominantly white labor force that issues a policy encouraging nepotism. In this case, even requesting information about friends and relatives could be construed as discrimination in certain situations. The only defense for this is job relatedness or business necessity.

IV. Devising a Nepotism Policy

Regardless of whether you support the practice of nepotism, you should develop a nepotism policy to define the hiring practices within your organization. This policy does not have to be complicated, but the following constituencies should be considered:

- Spouses
- Immediate family of employees (i.e., sons, daughters, brothers, sisters, parents and grandparents).
- Extended family (i.e., cousins, nephews, nieces, aunts, uncles, etc.).
- Friends
- Employees who marry each other

Developing the Policy

When writing a policy on nepotism, include the following:

- Definition of nepotism
- Hiring policy regarding the hiring of relatives and friends as compared to other candidates
- Employees who marry another employee
- Investigation of possible nepotism during the pre-employment process
- Penalties for misrepresenting relationships
- Hiring of temporary employees in relation to the nepotism policy
- Supervisory relationships between related employees

Word the policy carefully to avoid the implication of discrimination. Refusal to hire wives of employees, for instance, may be regarded as discrimination against women. The appearance of favoritism may attract the attention of the Equal Employment Opportunity Commission.

Recognize that seemingly neutral policies may have an adverse impact and get the company in trouble. Consult your attorney prior to implementation.

V. Tips on Screening Family and Friends

Deal with the hiring of family, friends and referrals in a fair and consistent manner. Consider the following hints:

Don't assume too much. Just because candidates come "highly recommended" from a relative or friend, don't assume they will fulfill your every want and need. Never hire sight unseen. The offer, "Send him over and I'll give him a job," has turned into disaster more than once. Interview the person thoroughly. Ask the same questions you would of a candidate you had never met before. Judge this person on the same criteria.

Interview the contact who referred the applicant. Determine whether the contact knows the candidate well enough to recommend him or her in good faith. Ask the reference some of the same questions you would ask the candidate.

Don't ignore references. Just because the candidate is being referred by someone you know, don't ignore other references that may be helpful. Former employers can offer special assistance in this situation. Chances are, the person who made the initial referral knows the candidate personally, not professionally.

Explain rejections to the references. While you are under no obligation to do so, an explanation of why a particular referral was rejected makes it clear that the person was treated fairly. This will insure that individuals within the organization will continue to provide referrals and not be discouraged by one rejection.

Exercise extreme fairness. Always err on the side of fairness when it comes to the hiring of family and friends. Any time a person of this nature is referred, you are probably being watched by a number of individuals within the company. You are under no obligation to hire anyone, but a little extra care in this process could go a long way.

Don't hesitate to investigate questionable situations. While you should be fair at all times, investigate what doesn't feel right. If you are not sure, for instance, why a particular person was referred, ask the person who referred him. There may be a specific situation they are trying to hide.

An applicant, for example, who has held four jobs in three years and comes "highly recommended" from Aunt Harriet may be a difficult employee. Ask the applicant the reasons for job changes and pursue it with his aunt as well.

Don't be influenced by outside sources. Be careful in allowing friends and family to influence your decisions. You know your needs better than anyone else. They probably have their own agendas. Family pressure may not have the company's best interests in mind.

Take existing employee relationships into consideration. Review the environment where a family member or friend will be placed. Will that person fit in? Are they going to feel comfortable working with these individuals? Examine, if possible, the ramifications of placing family members and friends into certain work environments. Placing a good friend of yours directly under a new manager, for example, may be perceived as a strategy to check up on the manager's performance.

Be prepared to address questions about your decision. Once again, you are under no obligation to do so. But a few well explained answers can smooth ruffled feathers when someone does not understand the circumstances and facts.

Make your expectations perfectly clear to the friend or relative if they are selected. While these individuals already understand the situation, make sure that they understand the expectations you have for the position. These criteria should not differ from any other person who would enter the job. Your selection does not allow them to work by a different set of standards.

If necessary, address the situation with existing employees. If you suspect there are uncertainties or grumblings about your selection, address the situation. Ask the parties concerned if they would like to air their feelings. The good will can go a long way toward building healthy communication.

Family members and friends should get "market salary" for the position they hold. Favoritism, especially when it comes to compensation, will be your undoing.

Family members should not participate in the hiring of relatives. Regardless of how competent these individuals may be, this practice leaves the management staff open to charges of conflict of interest and a host of other issues.

Family members should not supervise other family members. Once again, this practice leads to charges of conflict of interest and diminishing influence.

VI. The Nepotism Checklist

_____1. Have you reviewed your company's hiring practices to determine the number of family members and friends employed?

_____2. Has your company developed a nepotism policy?

_____3. Are the employees in your company encouraged to refer candidates for positions within the company?

_____4. Are all those who hire within the company aware of the nepotism policy and its practices?

_____5. Does your nepotism policy take anti-discrimination legislation into consideration?

Chapter 6

Evaluating Applications and Resumes

"I've never really done this before," he said. "We were always assigned receptionists from the pool. To be honest, I've never really hired anybody."

"I don't know what to tell you," she agreed. "All the resumes look the same and the only information I can get out of the references are job titles and dates of employment."

Here's What You'll Learn

Resumes have become the "business card" of job search. Every day millions are mailed or submitted in person to companies across the United States. An entire industry has grown up around the science of resume development and application completion. Hundreds of companies, colleges and counselors stake their reputation on "how to get inside the employer's head."

With the advent of computer technology, both applicants and employers are better able to manipulate the information they want to present or review. Those submitting resumes can now print them in color, send the over the internet, e-mail them to hundreds of employers at a time and customize them instantaneously.

On the other hand, employers can now scan paper resumes into a computer and eliminate a great deal of paper shuffling. At the same time, they can conduct a computer search to identify only those resumes containing specific terms, phrases, zip codes, degrees and so on. Unfortunately, what we have gained in efficiency, we have lost in personal attention to style and interaction. See the end of the chapter for more information on this topic.

What should you be looking for in one of these documents? Most applications and resumes provide a summary of experience, education, high school and college activities. They might begin with an objective that reads "a challenging and responsible career in the field of..."

Unfortunately this information can only provide a history of accomplishments (or lack thereof) and fails to inform the reader on what the applicant would do if given a position. This is not to say they are not somewhat helpful. By asking the right questions and looking for specific criteria, both an application and a resume may reveal some important facts about its owner.

I. Resumes and Applications: Where Should They Be Used?

While some companies use them interchangeably, resumes have been traditionally used for professional level positions. Applications have been commonly relegated to the areas of skilled, semi-skilled and non-skilled labor. In a few cases, larger companies have been using both.

While the application provides the same basic information as a resume, it does so in a rigid manner. Everyone completes the same information, in the same order and gaps in information are immediately apparent by blank space.

Resumes on the other hand, allow the author to express creativity when relating background. This is an opportunity to present the information in the priority in which the applicant thinks important. Resumes have been compared to advertisements in newspapers or magazines. Where do the eyes go? How is the information written to grab the most attention? Studies by job search experts indicate the average evaluator spends no more than 45 seconds in reviewing a resume before deciding the fate of its owner.

Both documents have their strengths and weaknesses. While resumes allow for creativity, one has to examine each resume more closely for the information needed to make a decision. The fact that a particular applicant lacks experience or training in a skill can be hidden in a morass of college activities, completed coursework and personal interests. Comparing resumes can be like comparing apples and oranges. They're both fruit and that's where the similarities end.

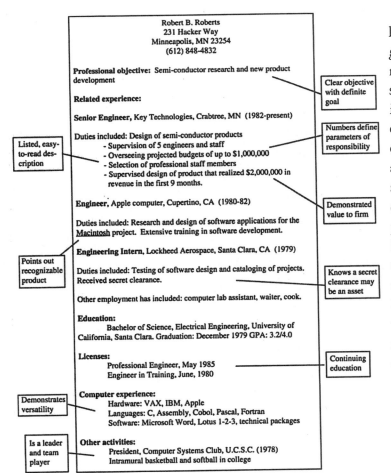

On the other hand, an application generally allows for no creativity whatsoever. While the information is listed, there is little opportunity for the applicant to demonstrate how much care went into preparation. With labor-oriented positions, a reflection of this caring may not be crucial. In positions where many forms of creativity are essential, the resume may serve as a harbinger of things to come.

93

II. Evaluating a Resume Effectively

What do you look for in a resume? This depends upon criteria determined ahead of time. Too often, evaluators look at a resume and discover an item they like: "Hey, he went to the same college and held a job as a waiter in high school just like me." There is an obvious empathy with someone who shares your experience and it can be tempting to include this person in the hiring process simply because of these extraneous facts. While a person's ability to fit into the new environment is important, sometimes too much emphasis can be placed on irrelevant details.

On the other hand, the resume may contain some details that the evaluator finds disheartening or inappropriate: "An English major! Why would anyone apply for a job as a processing manager if they were an English major?"

This person may be rejected simply over lack of identification with the applicant, but only based on the applicant's resume. Don't jump to conclusions.

Occasionally, you may be reviewing the resume of an acquaintance. This resume may have come from a referral or through an off-chance mention that the company was searching to fill a position. The temptation is to overlook certain shortcomings or mismatches for political reasons. The applicant may be a personal friend, or a friend of the boss. The evaluator may not want to face the possibility of having to reject that person and ruin a relationship.

Because of this, the evaluation of these resumes should be made with care. Many owners have experienced the consequences of ignoring their business sense in favor of a political situation.

The key to evaluating a resume is to remain impartial. This may be easier said than done, but the attempt must be made. Not only might you mis-hire, but, the legal aspects of these off-handed decisions may prove extremely expensive.

The requirements of the Immigration Reform and Control Act of 1986 are a good example. The guidelines for this law specifically state that an applicant may not be turned away simply because of the sound of his/her name. This, the law says, is clearly discrimination.

Prior to the review of any resume, the evaluator must have a clear picture of the position to be filled. This picture should be provided by

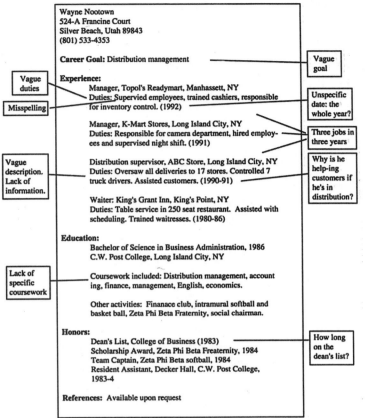

a job description and any other information deemed relevant. Place yourself in the successful applicant's position for a moment. What would this person need to know about the job duties, company culture and organizational rules and guidelines to excel in the job? When evaluating a resume, five areas need to be taken into consideration:

- Overall appearance
- Organization
- Education
- Experience
- Information concerning other relevant activities

Overall Appearance

The overall appearance of the resume gives you an indication of the care taken in preparation.

- Are there spelling errors?
- Is everything in the proper tense?
- Is the resume printed on a good quality bond with envelope and cover letter to match?
- Is the printing readable? (including style of typeface, and clarity of copy)
- What other criteria do you personally look for when reviewing something of this nature?
- Does it have that "textbook" appearance? Did the applicant write it or was it prepared by a professional?
- What impresses you positively and negatively?

While some of the items above may appear inconsequential, they indicate the level of care put into the resume and therefore the level of interest the applicant may have in doing a good job. When you are reviewing more than a hundred resumes, faded printing, poor quality paper, spelling errors and the like can be distracting.

Organization

- Does the resume tell you what you want to know?
- Has care been taken to include information that will help you in the decision making process?
- Does it ramble with no clear path or direction?
- Are the individual entries consistent and understandable?
- Do you find the information you need when looking under the logical category?

How a person organizes the information on a resume can provide insight into their priorities and their understanding of the position to be filled. It is common sense as an applicant to place yourself in the shoes of the employer and to decide how to organize the resume's content to make it most effective. Applicants who do this, show a caring and understanding of the process.

Some applicants place education above experience, for example, even though they have several years of related work. These individuals exhibit very little understanding about the importance of practical experience in pursuing a position.

The organization used in various explanations indicates the person's ability to communicate effectively. The length of explanations can be a reference to how talkative the person is and can also indicate their command of the English language. Make a list of other criteria to judge in the organization of a resume. How can these criteria relate to an applicant's ability to excel in the position?

Education

The evaluation of education can be fairly straightforward. It is important, however, to determine the educational requirements of the position in advance. While a college degree may be helpful in many cases, it is certainly not mandatory.

An evaluator needs to look at the motivations of an applicant who possesses more education than the position requires. With the number of college graduates each year, it is conceivable that no other work could be found. On the other hand, it is also quite possible that this same applicant will grow bored and unproductive in a short period of time in a non-stimulating job.

More than one company, large and small, has hired on the basis of most education, and has later been hurt by the turnover of that same employee. Matching education to job requirements can be a difficult issue, but one that needs attention.

Define what level of education is required for the job. Check the resume to ascertain the applicant's educational qualifications. Be flexible in this area since a particular major is not required in most cases. An applicant with an English degree might very well perform the job as capably as one with a degree in management. There are exceptions to this rule, such as accounting and engineering, but these are rare.

Regardless of qualifications, *check all educational credentials with the granting institution if you are serious about the candidate*! With the tightening job market, more individuals are claiming degrees and certifications they have not earned. These deceptions can be very damaging.

Experience

For most companies, an applicant's experience is critical information. There are exceptions to this of course, but having a previously skilled applicant certainly eases the situation.

Since it is rare that an applicant will walk through the door with identical experience to what you are seeking, the next best alternative is to compare the experience identified with your requirements. Job searchers are taught to assess their transferable skills so they may be explained on a resume or during an interview. While these may be laid out clearly on the resume, the evaluator should examine this information closely to verify a match.

When examining the experience section, consider the following:

- Do they provide parameters from which to judge responsibility? (number supervised, size of budget, amount of sales)

- Duties versus responsibility (What did they actually do?)
- Has the applicant thought about how his/her acquired skills will fit into the position sought? It's possible to be responsible for something and not know a thing about it.
- Do they provide a list of accomplishments which give an indication of work ethic and working knowledge of a discipline.
- Tenure in the position. "Manager" does not hold much water if they were in the position for three months.
- Is this the real job title? Applicants can be pretty free with descriptions and fool a lot of people. ("Well, I wasn't really the manager. But I did all the work and he just sat around.")

As with education, checking references is of great importance. More than one applicant has exaggerated their past or completely lied. Some experts estimate that 30% of all resumes in the market at any one time contain this type of false information.

When examining the experience section of a resume, the evaluator must at once be fair and strict. Remember that the experience detailed may have been significantly more involved yet the applicant was too modest to claim it. An example of this might be one who lists a job title such as "documents clerk" when the position involved much more than initially perceived.

On the other hand, some experience claimed might not have happened exactly the way it was described. This would be the person, for instance, claiming the title "manager" when in reality s/he was responsible for a small portion of a particular project. Yes, there was management taking place. But then a person who is in charge of anything or anybody might be considered a manager.

This same caveat holds true with other types of positions, especially dealing with technically related matter. It may look the same, but is it?

Determine in advance the personal characteristics of the ideal applicant for the position. A long tenure of employment with one company can have its pros and cons. Long-term may imply company loyalty, ability to get along with others and ability to contribute on a team. On the other hand, some of the energy and risk orientation toward one's job may have diminished along with the development of a certain sedentary quality.

A number of short-term employments can have a variety of meanings. The applicant could be moving quickly due to hard work and assertiveness. This might be just the type of person needed for a small company. But short-term employment could also mean lack of concentration, impatience or some other negative characteristics. A company "lucky" to land these new employees might lose them a short time later.

Other Activities

This category may carry a wide range of information. Community involvement, college activities, church related functions, hobbies and special interests all provide a glance into the type of person.

While in many cases, this information is not related to the applicant's ability to do the job, it may provide an opportunity to see potential for other possibilities in the future. Leadership positions in college activities usually provide at least some training as does involvement in professional associations. These experiences, although not formally compensated, translate well into strong skills.

Discriminatory Information

The appearance of discriminatory information on a resume is usually little cause for concern. However all individuals involved with the selection process should be aware that this type of information may not be included in the consideration of a candidate (no matter how helpful it may be).

Your company should develop a simple policy regarding this information if found on a resume. While the chances of a visit by the Equal Employment Opportunity Commission is remote, the burden of proof that they are not discriminating is generally left to the company. This can be an expensive legal nightmare. Some companies have a receptionist cross off the offending material with a magic marker before it reaches the evaluator.

III. Evaluating Cover Letters

Included with most resumes and applications is a cover letter from the job seeker. These documents can provide a variety of clues about their author with the help of the tips listed on the next page.

Tips for Review

Ask yourself the following questions when evaluating these works:

- Is it written in proper business format? Since this is a form of business correspondence, the letter should represent itself as such. Is it clean and crisp showing care has been taken in typing?
- Is there care shown in the preparation of the letter? Is it addressed to yourself or a person within your organization? Does the salutation read "Dear Sir"?
- Is it an original letter or are you one of 467 recipients? The best way to detect this is to look for referrals to your organization other than the canned phrases found in junk mail. If there is evidence to this effect, you can assume the applicant has researched your organization to some degree. This is a very positive sign since so few applicants choose to do so.
- How correct are the spelling and grammar? Is the letter written concisely?
- Does the letter achieve its objective? Does it impress you with the applicant's focus and reasons for wanting the job? Is it well organized?
- Finally, does it have that marketing quality that sells you on how the applicant can contribute to your organization?

Every evaluator has their own peculiarities when reviewing correspondence. The best policy is to go with your tendencies since you know the organization better than anyone else. (This of course has to be kept within reason. One employer will not review resumes and correspondence unless they are printed on white paper, period!)

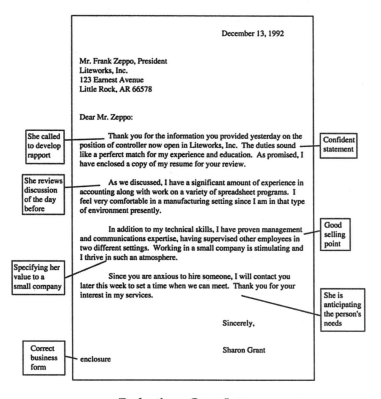

December 13, 1992

Mr. Frank Zeppo, President
Liteworks, Inc.
123 Earnest Avenue
Little Rock, AR 66578

Dear Mr. Zeppo:

[She called to develop rapport] Thank you for the information you provided yesterday on the position of controller now open in Liteworks, Inc. The duties sound like a perferct match for my experience and education. As promised, I have enclosed a copy of my resume for your review. **[Confident statement]**

[She reviews discussion of the day before] As we discussed, I have a significant amount of experience in accounting along with work on a variety of spreadsheet programs. I feel very comfortable in a manufacturing setting since I am in that type of environment presently.

In addition to my technical skills, I have proven management and communications expertise, having supervised other employees in two different settings. Working in a small company is stimulating and I thrive in such an atmosphere. **[Good selling point]**

[Specifying her value to a small company] Since you are anxious to hire someone, I will contact you later this week to set a time when we can meet. Thank you for your interest in my services. **[She is anticipating the person's needs]**

Sincerely,

Sharon Grant

[Correct business form] enclosure

Evaluating a Cover Letter

IV. Development and Review of Applications

Every company has developed an application of some sort to organize the hiring process. A person enters the office and is handed an application which s/he completes, returns to the receptionist and then waits for an interview.

This process has encouraged the creation of hundreds of application forms which are sold over the counter in much the same way as a "boiler plate" apartment lease. While these generic documents can save time in the short run, they may mean trouble. Most companies distributing this type of information do so nationally. Some organizations using these forms fail to realize that state and local labor laws do vary. What can be asked in one jurisdiction may be prohibited in another.

Developing an Application

The most efficient strategy for developing your company's application is to first assemble a collection of samples from other organizations. There are also a number of manuals and companies which can be used as sources. Review the application example on the following page.

As you review the various forms, make note of questions that would be appropriate for your purposes. While the samples will resemble each other in many ways, compare the different wordings and choose the best for your firm. *Remember!* Each question needs to be checked for its legality within your locale. (If, in the future, you begin operations in other states, the application will need to be checked against the laws of each state in which you operate.)

If your company has exceeded 14 employees, it falls within the jurisdiction of federal anti-discrimination laws. (See Chapter Two.) In fulfilling these requirements, the organization may need to comply with affirmative action recordkeeping. Note that questions related to these areas (sex, marital status, national origin, religion, disability) may be asked on the application but cannot be used in the consideration of candidates. You might develop a system for preventing the evaluator from incorporating this information. A detachable section for these questions on the application is one alternative.

Failure to comply with these laws can be costly and, they are sometimes easily overlooked. State authorities could also enter the case. It is best to be very careful.

Review of Applications

The advantages of having every applicant complete the same form is ease of comparison along with assuring that every candidate is treated consistently. This certainly saves time and increases accuracy. Then again, it is difficult to read anything into the preparation of the form. The evaluator should have a clear picture of minimum requirements for the position. There will always be exceptional applicants and those who fall within the gray areas of being marginally qualified. Having these requirements in writing discourages mistakes and confusions.

Consider education and experience for example. A candidate submitting an application with two years' experience for a job which

Digi-Lectric
Employment Application

** Read the statement below *before* completing this application. Complete the entire application.

Position desired_____

NAME	Last	First	Middle	Social Security No.

Street Address		City	State	Zip

Home Phone: Business Phone:	Referred by: (if applicable)
Relatives employed by Digi-Lectric?	Military Service? When?

* Do you have any physical handicaps which may hinder you from performing the job you have applied for?

EDUCATION

School	City	State	Dates Attended	Course of Study	Grad?

List professional licenses and associations:

** Discrimination because of age, sex, race, color, religious creed, national origin, ancestry, physical or mental handicap, or military status is prohibited by federal and state law. Please exclude any information which indicates the above characteristics. If you are hired, you will be required to provide verification of any information reported on this application.

*Equal Opportunity Employer

If you have a handicap and would like to be considered under our affirmative action program, please inform us. Relevant information provided will not subject you to discriminatory treatment. Digi-Lectric is a government contractor subject to Section 503 of the Rehabilitation Act of 1973 and is required to take affirmative action to employ qualified handicapped individuals.

EMPLOYMENT (this section abbreviated for example)

Employer name and address	Your position & duties	Dates of employ	Wages (40 hr)
Supervisor's name and position		Reason for leaving	
Employer name and address	Your position & duties	Dates of employ	Wages (40 hr)
Supervisor's name and position		Reason for leaving	

Additional remarks:

REFERENCES

Name	Name	Name
Address	Address	Address
Phone	Phone	Phone

Read Before Signing

I hereby certify that all information contained on this application is true and complete. I authorize Digi-Lectric to contact all sources necessary to verify this information. I understand that any misstatement or omission is sufficient grounds for immediate discharge.

Signature_____ Date_____

requires three might still be included if s/he also has one year of college coursework in that field. A well written job order (such as those explained in Chapter Three) which identifies education as a viable alternative eases the job of the evaluator.

Here are some key points to be considered when reviewing these documents:

Clarity

Cleanliness, legibility, and organization are factors influencing an evaluator's opinion of a candidate. A large number of corrected mistakes, for example, can be an indication of a applicant's level of care when working. The applicant may also be adjusting the information to make it more attractive.

Ability to Follow Directions

Check to see if the information provided answers the question. Does it make sense? It is logical?

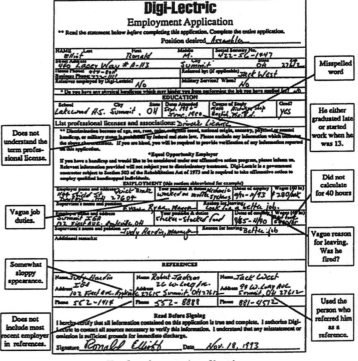

Evaluating an Application

Anyone who has dealt with employment applications can tell story after story of illogical answers, some rather humorous:

Q: Length of residence?
A: 75 feet.
Q: Have you ever been convicted of a crime?
A: Never been caught.
Q: Size of previous company?
A: 23 floors.

Accuracy of Information

- Does the information check out?
- Are there numerous spelling and grammatical errors?
- Do you have to work at deciphering the information offered?

As you might imagine, there are also numerous services on the market to analyze handwriting, color of ink, and the psychological implications of written responses. These will be discussed in Chapter Ten.

Remember that only those facts that are job related may be evaluated! A completed application, for example, may contain a number of spelling errors. This reason however, may not be used for disqualification of the candidate unless it can be shown that an ability to spell accurately is essential to the performance of the job.

V. Evaluating the Resume/Application/Reference "Package"

Once all information has been gathered on the applicants for a position, a decision must be made on who will be interviewed to receive closer scrutiny. The key to this process is organization and documentation.

The best way to handle decisions of this nature is to create a simple form with the pertinent criteria listed. Organization of this type will maintain fairness in the selection process and will also provide clear evidence in discrimination litigation. If this is a position that will be filled repeatedly, it pays to formalize the document and include it in procedural training. The form does not have to be complicated and should resemble the sample on the preceding page.

Decisions should be made with impartiality. Of course, there are exceptions. But these should be rare. Many smaller companies, for instance, develop a practice of hiring friends, relatives and other trusted associates in order to save money or to provide peace of mind. Time and time again, these hires eventually turn into difficult and expensive situations. (See Chapter Five.)

In the rush to hire new employees, the best laid plans can be overlooked. Documentation, organization and consistency are essential to smart hiring.

V. Resumes, Applications, and Technology

Advances in computer technology have resulted in the development of software programs that can assist employers in the collection and screening of both resumes and applications. Use of these programs can help eliminate some of the traditional paper shuffling that takes place in the selection process. Careful planning, however, is the key to using these advances. The options can be divided into four categories:

Resume Collection

This can be accomplished in several ways including a search of the World Wide Web, sending a broadcast e-mail to a group of people who may be interested in the position and simply posting the position on one or more electronic bulletin boards. There is no perfect way to do this since the Internet is in a state of continual change. (Consult Chapter Four for more specifics.)

Resume Screening

There are a number of firms now offering software which can electronically screen submitted resumes. These programs can be instructed to search for specific terms and phrases that an employer finds helpful. This, however, can prove counterproductive if suitable candidates are eliminated prematurely.

Application Completion and Screening

In addition to resume screening, some firms have developed software allowing applicants to sit at a computer terminal while completing the necessary information. This eliminates paper and allows the employer to manipulate the information in a host of ways.

Monitoring of EEO Requirements

These program generally come with the means for calculating and reporting on data pertaining to affirmative action efforts. In some cases, this software is integrated with the company's human resources information system.

Factors to Consider

Here are seven questions to ask when considering the use of resume and application screening software:

1. Does your company screen a volume of resumes and applications large enough to justify the expense and time for purchase and installation ?
2. Have you thoroughly investigated all software options available and the companies producing them? The approaches vary widely.
3. Is the software you are selecting upgradeable to new operating systems as they are introduced? If not, will the supplier modify the software to make it so? (Is that guaranteed?)
4. Is the software compatible with the network and software your company is presently using for other functions? Will the supplier allow you to verify this prior to purchase?
5. Have you visited with other companies using the software to see it in action and obtain their critique on its strengths and weaknesses?
6. How will the installation of screening software impact the quality and type of submissions you receive? (Critics observe that scanning devices work best with block letters on white paper, thus eliminating the opportunity for applicant creativity. This can also hold true with cover letters.)
7. Have you developed a method for monitoring the efficiency of the system once in place to determine whether its expense is justified.

As with any new technology, there are pros and cons. A good deal of this depends upon the computer literacy and acceptance of the technology from both applicants and employers. While these programs will continue to proliferate, the vast majority of application and resume gathering and screening will continue to be accomplished with traditional means.

Recordkeeping

It is essential to maintain accurate records on the application process to assure compliance with laws and to serve as a paper trail for future planning and recruitment. Because of the large numbers of resumes that pervade the workplace, there is a tendency among employers to discard resumes and applications of individuals not hired. Unfortunately some excellent candidates for the next job are lost in the trash.

Rather than review them here, a table of federal recordkeeping requirements for the hiring process is provided in Appendix B. It is best to consult your state's labor department for any additional laws.

VI. The Resume/Application Checklist

_____1. Have you examined the options of accepting resumes and applications? Which have you chosen and why?

_____2. Have you previously determined your selection criteria for reviewing resumes and applications? Be careful to make your selections based on these criteria. Be wary of letting non-job-related factors influence you.

_____3. When reviewing a resume, are you taking the five key areas into account: overall appearance, organization, education, experience, and other relevant activities?

_____4. When reviewing applications, and especially resumes, be diligent about checking facts. There is a great tendency among candidates to exaggerate qualifications.

_____5. Have you devised a system for screening out discriminatory information? (age, sex, marital status, national origin, religion, disability)

_____6. In reviewing cover letters, are you looking for the following qualities?

- Written in proper business format?
- Care shown in the preparation of the letter?
- Is it an original letter or one of 1000?
- Spelling, grammar, conciseness?
- Is it written with focus?

_____7. In developing an application, are you assembling a collection of others, reviewing them for good questions, designing your own and then having it reviewed for legality (especially concerning state laws)?

_____8. In reviewing applications, are you looking for the following qualities?

- Overall cleanliness, legibility, and organization?
- Did the applicant follow instructions?
- Do the responses answer the questions?
- Spelling and grammar?
- Does the information check out (dates add up, information consistent question to question, etc.)

_____9. When all the information has been gathered, are you handling the decision-making process with fairness and consistency?

_____10. Are you maintaining accurate records on the entire application process? A simple checklist might be designed to ease this task.

Applicant Screening Form

Position to fill_____Supervisor_____

As you review each application/resume, rate each of the characteristics below
according to the following scale:

1 = does not meet expectations
2 = meets expectations
3 = exceeds expectations
4 = outstanding

Decide on a cut-off point depending
upon your hiring goals.

Applicant	Educat.	Experien.	Appear.	Readable	Activities		Total

Note: It is strongly recommended that all <u>written</u> notes be destroyed after the selection has been made. More than one employer has gotten in trouble by writing down something that might appear to be discriminatory, such as "black woman" simply to help keep the applicants straight in their mind. While an innocent comment, it can be costly to defend.

Chapter 7

Screening Applicants by Telephone

"I'm calling about the job you have in the Post *this week," the caller said.*

"Oh yeah," responded the manager. "You mean that mechanic's job."

"Well it says diesel technician in the paper," said the caller.

"Right," retorted the manager. "So tell me about yourself."

"What do you want to know about?" asked the caller.

"The usual stuff," responded the manager.

Here's What You'll Learn

I. The Value of Telephone Screening

Other than resumes and applications, the initial telephone call to or from an applicant is the first real contact we have with that individual. While the amount of information we might obtain through a phone call is limited, there is still a tremendous amount we can gather about person's background, level of confidence, communication skills and a host of other things. Listening for the subtleties that they reveal about themselves as they talk begins to paint the picture you need for your evaluation.

But just as we are evaluating applicants, they are evaluating us. How was the phone answered? How long were they put on hold? Was the person they called prepared to answer their questions? Was the interviewer professional and courteous? Did the person seem rushed and harried?

As with any part of the applicant selection process, we are developing a relationship. Therefore, you must determine whether telephone screening will be a part of the selection process. To begin, let's look at the advantages and disadvantages of screening applicants via the telephone:

Advantages

- Screening over the phone is a faster process since each conversation tends to be shorter.
- It eliminates the hassles of scheduling, reserving rooms and the other tasks associated with formal interviews.
- Applicants can be screened as they call in, eliminating follow up calls.

Digi-Lectronics, Inc. Telephone Screening Form
for assembly and QC technicians

Remember:

- This call will be their first contact with Digi-Lectronics.
- Just as they want to make a good impression, we do too!
- Always keep a copy of the screening Evaluation with this form.
- Take your time and listen closely to the caller's answers.
- Listen to what they say and how they say it.
- Be sure to get a correct name, address and phone number, even if you don't think this person will be passed on to interviews.
- Be careful no to make commitments you can't keep.
- Do not invite callers in for an interview.
- We will make a decision within 48 hours and will be in touch if interested.

"The assembler's position involves putting together and soldering printed circuit boards that go into large electronic machinery. We have an opening on the _____ shift which runs from_____ to _____. The Quality Control technician inspects the work of the assemblers, but you need at least one year of electronic assembly experience to qualify."

Let me ask you a few questions about your qualifications:

Tell me about your work experience.

Where do you work now?

What are your duties?

How long have you worked there?

Why do you want to make a change?

Do you have any experience in working with electronics?

Hom much are you making right now? How much are wages and how much is incentive? (Do not discuss Digi-Lectronics' compensation at this point.)

Whay questions do you have about the job or Digi-Lectronics?

We will be making a decision in the next two days and will be back in touch if we would like to interview you further. Thank you for your interest.

COMPLETE THE EVALUATION FROM IMMEDIATELY

- Phones interview are viewed as less formal and therefore are more relaxed.
- The interviewer is not distracted by irrelevant factors such appearance, nervous habits, age, race and other discriminatory features.

Disadvantages

- Many of the non-verbal elements are lost, thus diminishing your ability to make an accurate judgment.
- While phone voice quality is excellent in most cases, static and extraneous noise can distract both the interviewer and applicant.
- Some people, by nature, do not communicate well over the phone. An interviewer or applicant who feels uncomfortable or is more visually oriented, may feel inhibited.
- Unless the interviewer has received an application or resume in advance, their ability to ask specific questions about an applicant's background and training can be difficult.
- It is easy for an applicant to avoid some situations since the interviewer cannot see non-verbal responses.
- Difficulty in reaching an applicant can create disfavor with the interviewer perhaps diminishing an applicant's prospects of making a good impression.

These factors and others more specific to your organization must be considered when deciding whether to screen applicant over the phone. A practical suggestion is to attempt it with one opening and the evaluate the results.

II. Preparing to Screen by Telephone

As you prepare for screening applicants, consider how they will apply. Will they submit resumes? Will they come in person to complete an application? Will they call upon seeing the job advertisement?

Having applicants call in may appear to be difficult and time consuming. But proper organization will enable you to shorten the actual screening process considerably.

Rather than sorting through resumes, applicants who call directly form the advertisement or posting can be screened immediately. Recognizing that 50 percent or more of applicants will be eliminated upon submission, taking five to ten minutes to screen each person as they call may eliminate a good deal of effort later on. The form on this page can be used as a format for preparing for phone-in applicants.

Here are a few suggestions if you choose to screen applicants over the phone after accepting applications:

Know the job. If you supervise the position, this is taken for granted. If, on the other hand, you screen for a number of positions, you may want to reacquaint yourself with the job's current duties and responsibilities.

Develop clearly worded questions and outline what you expect for answers. Try these questions on a few people inside the company to make sure the questions and understood and elicit the type of answers you seek.

Obtain input from those who will work with the new person. Even if you supervise the position being filled, you will not be the only person to work with the new hire. Soliciting suggestions and input from others will yield some good ideas and build their investment in hiring the right person for the job.

Prepare an evaluation form that will be used for all applicants. Notes on a legal pad will not provide the same clarity as a form which gives a summary of experience in the same place for each applicant.

Prepare what you will say about the job and organization when screening applicants. The best applicants for any position are talking with more than one employer. How well you represent the job and your organization may determine the quality of the applicants who show sincere interest in working for you.

Prepare for the common questions. Brainstorm a list of questions that applicants are most likely to ask. Your preparation will put them at each and demonstrate that you are truly concerned about hiring the right match for the job.

Rehearse the screening process. Take the time to call a couple of co-workers and go through the process to iron out glitches.

Appearing well prepared will make a positive impression on the best candidates.

Block out a time to screen applicants so you will not be interrupted. Nothing can be more infuriating to an applicant than to be continually put on hold so the interviewer can handle other details. What's worse is to have someone conducting other business or completing paperwork while attempting to conduct the interview. Respect shown to applicants will help lure the best to your business.

III. Reception of Call-in Applicants

The reception applicants receive when they first respond to a job notice is critical to beginning the process on the right foot. A person answering the phone who does not appear to know anything about the job can cause great harm in the way the company is perceived by those applying. Here are a few tips for ensuring that applicants are accorded the proper attention:

Prepare the receptionist. With all the distractions a receptionist deals with during the normal day, it is easy to understand how fielding calls from applicants may not seem important. Take the time to explain how critical first impressions are when attracting new employees.

Provide a prompt sheet for the receptionist. Give the person clear instructions on what to say and how to refer applicants to the proper person. A sample prompt sheet is provided on this page.

Obtain name, address and telephone number of every applicant. Regardless of whether the person is hired, every person who applies should have their vital information recorded. In some cases, that may be a legal requirement such as maintaining affirmative action logs. In other cases, there may be additional openings in which previous applicants may have an interest.

How to Handle Incoming Callers
for Digi-Lectronics job openings

Remember that this call will be their first contact with Digi-Lectronics. Just as they want to make a good impression, we do too!

Ask for what position they are applying.

Ask for name, address and telephone number.

Ask for the best time for an interviewer to reach them.

Ask where they heard about the job.

If a referral, get the referral's name.

Tell them that an interviewer will return the call within 24 hours.

Refer any questions they may have to the interviewer.

Make sure each call is handled professionally. Reinforce the receptionist's skill at answering the phone. By providing some positive feedback, that person is more likely to treat those calling you with more respect and friendliness.

Walk it through with the receptionist. If you're still not sure that your receptionist understands, try giving a couple of sample situations just to see how they are handled. In some cases, you may have a couple of friends call in as applicants just to see how they are received.

IV. Conducting the Screening

We hope that hiring anyone is going to be the beginning of a long-term relationship. Both the organization and the applicant are making a big commitment. It is critical therefore, that you make the most of every screening situation. Here are some tips for maximizing the way you can screen applicants on the telephone:

Develop rapport. Just as you would in a formal interview, take a minute to put the applicant at ease when you call. You might begin by asking how they found out about the job. If it was a referral, you might get into a short chat about that person.

Explain the position's duties up front. Begin the interview by telling the applicant about the position and how it fits within the organization. Ask the applicant to comment on ways their background fits the job as you ask some questions.

Take notes. Do not rely on your memory to recall all the information the applicant gives you. Jotting down a few key words here and there will help you complete the evaluation form at the end of the interview. You might also jot down follow up questions as they come up during the conversation.

Listen to what the applicant says and how it is said. While you listen to the words, look for level of confidence, organization of thought, consistency of focus. Even though the person is not sitting in front of you, there are still many ways you can pick up on communication signals.

Treat everyone the same. While you will identify with some applicants more than others, all applicants should receive the same level of attention and consistent message. Simply because you went to the same high school does not mean they should get special treatment, especially if they're not right for the job.

Ask everyone the same questions. It is easy to wander off the mark, especially if you get engrossed in a particular topic. It will become difficult however to make clear comparisons when you have gathered partial information on some applicants. Take the time to pursue items you think are important, but be sure to cover all the topics you need to.

Take your time. Applicants can detect whether or not you're in a rush. While you may have a million things on your mind, taking the time to concentrate on them will produce a better interview and demonstrate that you really do care about who you hire.

Question inconsistencies in what the applicant says. Do not hesitate to ask about comments that appear inconsistent. Those who shy away from potentially uncomfortable situations lose the opportunity to truly screen the best people into the rest of the process.

Use silence as a tool. One of the most powerful strategies any interviewer has is silence. Since most people are uncomfortable with a long silence, they tend to reveal more than they had planned. Sometimes the answer after the silence is more to the point.

Take time to answer the applicant's questions. While there will be more time to answer questions if they make it in to the formal interview stage, it is still important to answer the concerns of all applicants. In a few cases nervous applicants has changed the opinion of an interviewer because they asked such penetrating inquiries.

Don't make commitments you can't keep. Be careful not to promise an interview as a way of getting off the phone or answering a pestering question. You must remain in control of the interview. More than one employer has gotten in trouble by making a promise that was undeliverable.

Explain the rest of the selection process. Before closing the conversation, be sure the applicant understands what's next. One of the greatest sources of irritation for applicants is not knowing when or how a decision will be made. Remember, applicants are also customers.

V. Evaluating Applicants

Once each screening call has been completed, it is essential that the information be recorded immediately. The hustle of most businesses combined constant distractions make us forget most of what we hear within a couple of hours. Here are some quick tips for making the most of the information you gather:

Complete the evaluation immediately. Remain seated and fill out the form as best you can. Waiting to fill out two or three applicants' information at the same time will make the information run together.

Be consistent in evaluating. While there may be a tendency to be more generous with those applicants you liked, this has to remain a business decision. Their ability to get along well with others should be noted for instance, but not given undue weight. On the other hand, a person with excellent qualifications should nor be penalized if he appeared nervous on the phone if dealing with people is not a significant portion of the job.

Write complete thoughts. A jotted note here and there cannot be easily recalled two or three days later. The quality of your notes will have a direct impact on your ability to make an accurate decision.

Confine your comments to business necessity. Remain focused on how well the applicant matches the job requirements. The fact that he would make a great shortstop for the company team is irrelevant. Besides being inappropriate information to record, it could also be questioned should your notes be reviewed during a discrimination complaint.

Be careful what you write. In addition to irrelevant material, take care to avoid comments that would infer discrimination. The words "elderly

Telephone Screening Evaluation		
Name of applicant_____ Address_____ Applying for _____ Phone_____ Interviewer_____ Date _____		
Place your ratings for this candidate in the categories indicated. (Rating: 1 = Unacceptable, 5 = Exceeds expectations)		
	Comments	**Rating**
Work Experience		
Skills		
Education Training		
Electronics Experience		
Present Wages		
Other		
	Total Score =	

woman" written on an evaluation simply to help you keep the many applicants apart, could be questioned as biased against those covered by the Age Discrimination in Employment Act.

Follow through on commitments you made to the applicant. Once the evaluation has been completed, make sure to send any information you promised the applicant along with investigating questions they asked for which you had no immediate answer. Your prompt follow-up demonstrates your commitment to hiring the best.

VI. The Telephone Screening Checklist

1. Do you have a clear understanding of the job for which you are screening?
2. Have you developed a set of questions which reflect what you need to know?
3. Have you developed an evaluation form for screening applicants?
4. Have you reserved a block of time for screening applicants without interruption?
5. Have you prepared what you will say about the company?
6. Are you prepared for the common questions applicants will ask?
7. Have you prepared the receptionist to receive applicants' incoming phone calls?
8. Do you question inconsistencies during the interview?
9. Do you ask each applicant the same questions?
10. Do you refrain from making commitments?
11. Do you complete the evaluation form for each applicant immediately after the screening?

Take Charge
Interviewing

"But what is it about this person that makes you so sure we should offer her a job?" asked Frank.

"It's a feeling in my gut," said Steve. "I've never interviewed such a fantastic candidate before."

"Who was interviewing whom?" asked Frank. "I can't go upstairs and say 'Let's hire Susan because Steve's got a fantastic feeling in his gut.'"

Here's What You'll Learn

I.	Detecting the Winners
II.	Establishing the Process
III.	Developing Questions
IV.	Conducting the Interview
V.	Alternative Interview Strategies
VI.	The Interview Checklist

What is it about interviews that makes us think we can "wing it"? Maybe its the chemistry we feel with the applicant. Maybe it's their appearance. Perhaps we're overwhelmed by their insight and maturity.

On the other hand, maybe we just don't have time to really prepare. Maybe we're distracted with ten other tasks. Maybe we just don't care enough.

Interviews must be conducted with care and diligence. We often rely too heavily on the results of interviews and mistakes are made in the final employment decision.

I. Detecting the Winners

There are essentially three goals when conducting an employment interview:

1. To develop an *accurate* picture of the job for which you are hiring and communicate that to each applicant.
2. To collect enough information on the applicant to make an informed decision.
3. To produce a positive and accurate picture of the company—one that will impress applicants and help them decide to work for you.

But how do you detect the winners among those who apply?

Collecting information on an applicant is a complex task. It must be done methodically and with premeditation. Even experienced interviewers find it easy to get caught up in the charisma of some individuals. While chemistry plays a role in this process, a good interviewer will stick to the plan.

Just as some applicants will impress you, others may turn you off. One must be careful not to judge too soon. If you have conducted employment interviews, you've probably followed the traditional method of asking questions and receiving answers for 30-60 minutes and then asked if the candidate had any questions. Much of your evaluation was probably based on emotion and impressions developed in the first five minutes.

While this is the primary method used in business, that doesn't necessarily make it the most effective. A good number of candidates feel comfortable in this format and prepare well for the expected questions. In fact, the slicker of these candidates don't necessarily prepare. But they can impress you with their answers even if they don't have the necessary qualifications for the job.

Other candidates might be excellent possibilities for the opening but they just don't interview well. You may be one of these individuals. How do you feel in these situations?

Ability to "perform" in an interview should be only one consideration in employee selection. Part "V" of this chapter introduces some effective alternatives to the simple question and answer session.

II. Establishing the Process

The first step for developing an interview process is to evaluate the position you are filling, and then determine the information needed to make an accurate decision. You then tailor the questions to address those needs.

If you are hiring a salesperson, for example, you will need to know that the successful candidate is persuasive, self-motivated, well organized and affable. If you are hiring an assembly technician, you will look for someone with an orientation to detail, good levels of concentration with an ability to follow instructions.

You personally, may have an orientation towards good communicators and will therefore look for those candidates who are conversationalists. But if you're hiring a production worker, a good conversationalist is apt to get less accomplished. However, you would not hire a shy and retiring individual to represent the company in sales.

Recognize that the best person to hire is someone who finds the job challenging and is able to do the majority of it upon entering the company. A good rule of thumb is to select someone who can do 80% of the job. Therefore this person has room to grow, yet he/she is not starting from the beginning.

Interview Priority Checklist

Position_____ Dept. _____

In developing and effective interview process for this position, list the skills and characteristics you feel are most important for a successful candidate. Make sure all are job-related. When this form is complete, use the information to develop questions and the structure of the interview. Weigh each skill or characteristic according to its level of importance: 1=low, 5=critical.

Priority	Skill/Characteristic	Weight
	Total Weight	

Be careful not to hire individuals who are too much like yourself. While the two of you may get along very well, the is the potential for ensuing power struggles, and group think. Hire someone who will challenge you in the position, but from a standpoint of growth. This way the person compliments your strengths with theirs. If you are a practically oriented person for instance, hiring someone with creativity is a nice compliment.

Review the job description before developing the list of criteria. Observe the successful individuals that currently hold the position and others like it in your organization. What makes those people excellent employees? How have they developed? What were they like when first hired? You might even ask them what they would look for in a good candidate for a position like theirs.

Another strategy is to bring together those who are working in the department and ask them, "Now that Richard has left, what qualities who you like to see in the new person that Richard did not have? Then ask, "What qualities would you like to see in the new person that Richard did have? and Finally ask, "What qualities did Richard have that you would not like to see in the new person? This strategy provides you with valuable input and gives those in the department an opportunity to contribute to the new person's selection.

Rarely will you be able to find a candidate that has the training, maturity and natural smarts to become productive immediately. If you do, they may not be affordable. Everyone has to be trained. *Set your criteria for individuals who will grow into the job.*

This holds true for every position, from production to customer service to executive levels. Hire totally trained specialists only when absolutely warranted. These individuals tend to be expensive, may have their own agenda, and can be difficult to work with. A person who matures into a job has more investment in the outcome.

Taking Diversity into Account

As the labor force continues to change, employers are facing new challenges and opportunities. The stereotypes about hiring only white males under forty are disappearing due to that group diminishing in size. Forward looking employers are taking advantage of these changes by targeting the new diverse groups in the work force.

Women have been a major factor for years in the labor force. Their role has expanded dramatically as they assume more responsibility. While discrimination and bias are widely prohibited, it is still very much in practice throughout the nation. Employers who are continually successful in hiring and retaining the best, use diversities to their advantage rather than discriminating against them. These other diversities include people of color, immigrants, senior workers, and the disabled. Your ability as an employer to adjust to these groups and to take advantage of their interests experience and work ethic will serve to strengthen your standing within the industry and community.

The greatest challenge facing some employers is the growing number of applicants unable to speak English. While some argue that English should be the only language spoken on the work site, reality indicates you, the employer, must be able to communicate clearly with all employees if for no other reasons than safety. An employer's willingness to work toward a common solution not only increases communication but demonstrates flexibility and an orientation toward teamwork.

In addition to language barriers, other challenges exist such as differences in cultural heritage, levels and types of education, experience, and balance of life issues. When interviewing candidates, all of these factors enter in regardless of whether the employer is aware of it. Applicants are hiring you as much as you are hiring them. Therefore your ability to communicate care and sincerity about their welfare is of paramount importance. If you are dealing with applicants of diverse backgrounds, consider what you are doing to accommodate them during the interview process. Place yourself in their shoes and consider their concerns and apprehensions about your hiring process. Keep a list of factors such as language barriers, cultural concerns, reading levels, the understanding of language nuances and social norms, appearance and dress and the like. Then strive to address each one of these issues.

Process Factors

A smooth flowing process is essential to making each interview effective. Here are a few factors to consider:

Urgency of the need. How fast does the position need to be filled? The more urgent, the less care can be allowed in selection.

Level of the position. You will probably spend more time in the selection of supervisors than receptionists. However the latter should still be accorded proper attention. Rushing them through an interview says "you're not that important." Front-line people can make or break an organization.

Industry trends. While some industries attempt to reduce turnover, others accept it as a fact of doing business. Food service and retailing are good examples of the latter. Examine your level of turnover. Is it worth reducing? Balance recruiting costs with training costs.

Taking great care in the selection process only to have these individuals leave after three to five months is probably not the best use of your time. If you are expecting high turnover, your questions are going to be based more on attendance, punctuality and work ethic than on why candidates are interested in the position and their five year goals.

Available labor pool. Economic conditions, along with the demographics in your area may determine the type of interviewing you can conduct. In a tight labor market, for instance, you may find that you're forced to ease some criteria just to fill certain positions.

If the area's demographics indicate a high level of education and you're running an assembly plant, you may hire locally and expect turnover (due to lack of challenge) or recruit from several towns away in a labor-oriented community. While turnover may decrease in the latter, you may also have to pay a travel differential.

These four factors, in conjunction with established job criteria, dictate the design of the interview process.

Make Them Work

Most candidates are not made to work in the interview. They arrive expecting the obvious questions and are usually right on target: "Why do you want this job? Tell me about your experience? Why did you leave your last job?" And so on.

Richard Bolles, author of the job search bestseller, *What Color is Your Parachute?*, compares this technique to reading tea leaves, trying to tell the future from the past. Unfortunately, the level of accuracy for this is dismally low.

Allowing candidates to slide through on the expected procedure works against you. The best candidates will enjoy the challenge. Ask tough questions. It shows you care about who fills the position.

Focus on Behaviors Rather Than Fact and Opinion

Anyone can tell you what they think is best way to handle a difficult customer, for instance. It is another thing to have done it successfully. Many applicants are getting better and better at giving pat answers to the predictable questions. But one can't afford to simply accept what people say at face value. There are too many books on the market now that tell them what to say.

Instead of asking the predictable questions, you might ask the person to tell you a story about a time when s/he had to deal with a difficult customer. What was the situation? How did the person attempt to handle it? What was the result? What did the person learn? Even if the situation related was not handled successfully, there is plenty to learn about the applicant.

The way a story is told allows insight into the person's poise, attitude, and ability to communicate. You might also discover insights into their personal priorities and strategies for problem solving. If you listen closely, you can also check on the consistency of the information given. It the applicant is fabricating the story, you can usually tell because of details they omit or details that appear strange or inconsistent. Once the story has been told, you can go back and verify what sounds unusual.

Use phrases like, "Help me understand..." or "I'm a little confused. Could you explain...", when challenging the accuracy of what the applicant has said. While something may appear to be a bold-faced lie on the surface, there may be a perfectly reasonable explanation for what the person said. Check it out first. If, in fact, the person is lying, waste no time in ending the interview.

Defining the Process

Design an interview process that is easy to follow and does not include too many steps. Too much information can be just as damaging as too little.

Limit the number of people interviewing candidates. In many cases one is sufficient. The more involved the tougher it is to make a decision.

Each candidate should be interviewed the same way. Questions, exercises and tasks should not vary and all should be job-related.

Be careful not to build marathon schedules. Candidates interviewed late in the afternoon tend to suffer in evaluations. This helps neither them or you. Try to schedule interviews in the morning when everyone is fresh.

Give candidates a chance to catch their breath. Three, hour-long sessions back to back would exhaust anyone.

Only interview the best and limit the number. Meeting with 20 candidates because you cannot decide between resumes exacerbates the problem. The first round should not include more than six people. The second round should be limited to three and the third round (if absolutely necessary) should be limited to two. More than three rounds of interviews becomes counterproductive.

Stay on time and follow through. A normal selection process should consume no more than three weeks from the deadline for applications. Clerical positions should take much less. Applicants stew over the selection decisions a company makes. In waiting too long, you may lose the best candidates.

Think back about the last interview you conducted. Did you prepare as if your livelihood depended on it? In some ways, it does!

III. Developing Questions

The questions selected and how they are formed are the most important element of an interview. Each question must address defined criteria for the job. Simply asking random questions to "get to know the person" will not suffice.

The inquiry should be understandable and specific, while leaving the candidate an opportunity to elaborate. Each question should be tested before being used. Ask a sampling of employees if they understand it? Is it clear? Is it too long? Should it be broken into two pieces?

Emphasis should be placed in various areas depending upon the position available. Questions about education should take a back seat to skills and abilities when interviewing laborers. Asking a carpenter about college education is irrelevant and may be discriminatory.

When developing questions, be sure they are job-related and non-discriminatory. Innocent mistakes can be costly.

Categories of Questions

What questions can you ask in an interview? These fall into five categories:

- Career goals/occupational objectives
- Education
- Work experience
- General skills and aptitudes related to job criteria
- Attitudes and personality characteristics

Career Goals/Occupational Objectives

The purpose here is to determine candidates' focus and determination. Why do they want the job? What makes it so special? Ask for specifics. What is their philosophy? Does the person sound like they believe what they're saying?

This category is relative, however. Asking a fry cook for goals and objectives may not yield as much valuable information as facts about work history and skills.

Focus on the behaviors and actions the applicant describes. Can you see a pattern of career direction or does the person seem to be accepting any job offered?

Education

Education should not play a large role in the interview unless there is little job-related work experience to discuss. You may still be able to gain some insight by examining extracurricular activities in addition to academics.

Work Experience

The majority of time should be spent on the applicant's previous experience, especially that which is directly related to the new position. Look for specifics. Simply having a candidate outline what they did may not be enough. Examine how well they performed the job, how much training was involved and why they left.

Look beyond the job title. Many titles can be misleading. What is it that they actually did?

Ask what improvements they made on the job. What made them stand out? Ask about their boss and colleagues. How did they get along?

General Skills and Aptitudes Related to Job Criteria

Learn what actual skills an applicant will contribute to the job. How skilled is this person? Have they worked with your materials and/or machinery before? Are they familiar with procedures? Can they demonstrate these skills?

Have applicants read aloud during the job interview. By doing so, they will demonstrate two things: 1) Their actual ability to read and 2) their level of confidence. Be careful however to only ask them to read materials required on the job. A good example of this would be asking a housekeeper to read the safety labels on cans of cleaning fluid.

Once again, you have to be specific in your questions. The fact that an applicant says he can do something is not always correct. He may be exaggerating. Check everything out.

Attitudes and Personality Characteristics

How well does this person get along with others? Will he fit into your working environment? You can pick up a great deal of information about these characteristics by just listening to his answers to other questions.

Is he stubborn? Does he get angry? Does he like his current occupation? Is he satisfied? Did he leave his last employer under difficult circumstances? All of these considerations and others will give you a better idea of whether this person will fit into your organization.

NOTE: A collection of 500 sample questions for all five categories can be found in Appendix A.

IV. Conducting the Interview

An employment interview should be a well-planned exercise. The interviewer should prepare by assuring that proper attention is accorded the meeting. If conducted as an after-thought in a busy day, the results will most likely be dismal. Care and time must be invested to make these sessions a success.

Prepare the Location

An interview involves more than just the questions. It also includes the environment in the person will work. Take a walk around your work site. Examine the general appearance. Are there overflowing trash cans, lights out, or a look of disorganization? Is there a separation between executive and staff washrooms, executive parking spaces and other signs of class distinctions? Look at the bulletin boards. What messages stand out? Are there signs for employee get together and information or is it filled with corporate directives? Does anyone read it?

Fourteen Tips to Screening

Review the candidate's application materials. You have already seen it once, but review it again. Having to repeatedly refer to these papers during the interview is distracting and indicates a lack of preparation.

Prepare the location. If it's your office, be sure things are in order. There should be no interruptions during the interview. If this is impossible, find an alternate location.

If a plant or office tour will take place, make sure it has been properly arranged.

Put the candidate at ease. Seemingly insignificant gestures can go a long way toward setting the right tone for an interview. Meet the applicant on time. Don't make them wait. Ask your secretary, in the presence of the candidate to hold calls. When opening the interview, make the candidate feel comfortable. Offer a cup of coffee. A little small talk never hurts.

Outline the interview. Explain the sequence of events to define the parameters of what will happen. Resist the urge however, to identify a time frame. A defined 45 minute interview may be difficult to end after 15 minutes if things are not going well.

Keep an open mind. First impressions of a candidate are usually lasting. Try not to prejudge the candidate based on the first 30 seconds of contact. Nervousness and other factors may be obscuring the better qualities.

Interview Evaluation

Applicant_____ Phone_____

Applying for_____ Supervisor_____

Interviewer_____ Date_____

Instructions: List in priority order the required and preferred skills and characteristics for the job based on the interview priority form. When this has been accomplished, make a copy of the completed form for each candidate to be interviewed.

Indicate only numerical ratings on this form when evaluating a candidate. Arrange the interview questions so that all areas listed on this form are addressed. The questions do not have to be in order.

Ratings: 1= Unacceptable for this position 5= Exceeds requirements

Required Skills/Characteristics	Weight
Total Weight	

Preferred Skills/Characteristics	Weight
Total Weight	

Let the candidate do the talking. Resist the temptation to converse. Ask questions and wait for answers. Interviewer silence can be a powerful tool for eliciting additional information.

Be attentive. When conducting a series of interviews, boredom can overtake you, along with distractions about more pressing problems. Concentrate on what is being said. This may be the only opportunity you have to evaluate this candidate.

Observe body language. In addition to what is being said, watch and listen to how it is being said. Is there a level of enthusiasm? Does the person sound confident? Do they make eye contact?

Take notes. As the interview progresses, record responses and impressions for later reference. When interviewing more than one candidate, information will blur together. These notes will help sort it out.

Maintain control. Be careful not to let the interviewee take over. An aggressive candidate may attempt to get the better of you by making comments or asking questions, rather than answering. In other situations, the session may appear to be going so well, you lose track of time and organization.

Probe incomplete answers. There may be a reason why answers are incomplete. Ask for clarification, even if it is difficult or embarrassing. You need to know.

Test for character. After a person has given the answer to a question, ask about their approach and reasoning. Ask them how much they would be willing to bet if they think they are correct. Testing their confidence can be very revealing.

Keep reactions to yourself. The so-called "poker face" is useful in an interview. Be careful not to display your emotions, regardless of how pleased, shocked, disappointed, or frustrated you may be. Signals such as these give candidates an impression, perhaps wrong, of how they're doing.

Interviewer's Self Rating Sheet

Applicant interviewed_____ Date_____

Evaluation:
5 = Handled smoothly
4 = Handled well, but needs refining
3 = Has a grasp but needs improvement
2 = Needs significant work
1 = Found this difficult

Rapport with the Applicant

Opened the interview and made the applicant feel at ease	____
Avoided direct criticism of the applicant	____
Listened sympathetically	____
Put applicant at ease in awkward situations	____

Control of Interview

Developed questions in advance of the interview	____
Maintained the focus of the interview	____
Made smooth transition from one topic to another	____
Allocated time appropriately	____
Returned to the original question when answer evasive	____
Paced interview well	____

Persuaded applicant to elaborate on responses using:

Follow up questions	____
Silence	____
Paraphrasing applicant's initial response	____

Note Taking

Took notes discreetly during interview	____
Did not allow note-taking to interfere with interview	____
Noted dress and appearance if relevant	____

Take lunch in a comfortable setting. Take the applicant to a place where the employees usually go for lunch. A more relaxed restaurant results in a more relaxed candidate.

Close the interview on a positive note. The candidate may or may not have an idea of how the interview went. Refrain from announcing a decision. Assure the candidate that you will be in touch within a short period of time and thank him for his time.

Write an interview summary. Immediately after the interview, write down your general impressions and review your notes. Waiting even one hour will greatly reduce your memory of what took place.

V. Alternative Interview Strategies

There are a number of alternatives to the standard question-and-answer session. These make the candidate work harder for the position. The work s/he produces in these exercises is a much better indicator of success on the job. Different strategies work for different needs. Consider the following:

Conduct the interview while giving a tour. It is best to observe applicants in the organizational environment. Interviewing someone in the office can create a sterile and, in some cases, uncomfortable atmosphere.

As you tour, begin by explaining how the different areas of the organization work. Add in some statistics and interesting facts about the company. Try to make the tour fascinating. Fascinated people tend to work harder.

Watch the applicant for level of interest and attention. Does the person ask questions? Do they appear distracted? Do they look uneasy or intimidated?

Next, take the person "behind the scenes." Explain the workings of inventory, computer system, and other functions that are pertinent to your situation. Stand on the dock and ask them a few questions. Take them into the production area. Show them how the creative department works.

As you do this, slip in some questions about them. What's their background? Where did the person last work? Why did they apply to your? You might also ask them to relate a story about how they dealt with a particular situation in another job. Doing this while on a tour tends to relax people. In many cases, the applicant will offer information and insights they may have held back in a more traditional interview.

As you give this tour, introduce the applicant to a number of staff. How does the applicant respond? Does the person make eye contact? Does s/he appear intimidated by strangers? Would employees or customers mind approaching this individual with a question?

A tour can provide you with observations of eye contact, energy level, posture, level of self esteem, and apparent interest in the position. It's one thing to say you're interested. It's another to act interested. Having introduced each applicant to people on your team, you can also solicit the team's feelings about each person. After all, they have to work with whomever you select.

Interview project. Ask the candidates to complete a project during the interview to get a sampling of their work. Evaluation of this work would include organization, cleanliness, and written skills in addition to content. You might ask a sales management applicant, for instance, to develop a short marketing plan based on your criteria.

Homework assignment. An expanded variation of the above would ask applicants to take the assignment home, develop the necessary material, and return it within two or three days. You could then review it with them.

Make a presentation. After a candidate has completed either of the above, you might ask for a presentation on the material completed. If the position requires the person to make presentations as a normal duty, this will serve as an excellent means for evaluating those skills. Candidates might also make presentations on their goals, how they would attack the job, how their background would enhance the position or a host of other topics.

Provide typical situations. Candidates can be asked to respond to a variety of daily occurrences. To solve these situations, they might have to write a memo, conduct research, interview others, hold a meeting or a combination thereof. While this exercise is probably not appropriate for clerical positions, it can clearly demonstrate the skills and abilities of managerial candidates.

This type of assessment takes time and preparation. But if you are interested in hiring the best for your organization, this investment is well worth it.

Interview minutes. Have each candidate write up minutes of the interview after it has taken place. These minutes can indicate how much interest the candidate has in the position by the care taken in their preparation. On the other hand, minutes dashed off in 15 minutes may indicate that the person is a producer. Candidates who do not fare well in a face to face interview may demonstrate their skills in the minutes they write.

Internships. For those candidates still in college, an internship in your company benefits all. The student gains practical experience and skills and you have the opportunity to take a long look at a potential employee. The only caveat is that hosting an intern takes some time and preparation. These are not simply warm bodies to do the filing.

Assessment Centers. An assessment center consists of a series of exercises performed over a day long period which measures a person's ability to perform specific tasks. The evaluation is conducted by experienced managers. For managerial applicants, this center might consist of an in basket exercise, a group project involving all of you top candidates and a presentation to other managers. For a non-managerial position the center might consist of a project involving organization of materials, a report to be developed and a series of letters to be written or typed. While more time consuming, the accuracy of this process has been proven time and again.

Full- or half-day trials. This strategy gives them the opportunity to get to know the members of the team with which they will be working. Look for chemistry, ability to communicate, personal organization and other factors essential to the position they would be filling. If there are specific skills necessary, be sure they are required to demonstrate these skills some time during the day.

Video-tape interviews. Prepare a list of questions in advance and have each of your top candidates asked these questions on tape. This method allows for direct comparisons between applicants.

Computer assisted interviews. A few companies have developed computer driven interviews in which each candidate answers questions asked by a computer. The computer asks questions based on the candidate's previous answers. The candidate may also be asked to type in a response to a particular situation. Companies using this process have found a higher level of motivation in candidates using this system. This system allows employers more consistency in obtaining information and remaining unbiased.

Targeted selection systems. For an improved approach to the traditional interview, a targeted selection process can be very effective. Instead of asking questions such as "Tell me about yourself," the targeted question asks for information on a particular skill or experience. For example:

"This job involves a good deal of customer service problem-solving. Please tell me about an experience you've had where you dealt successfully with an angry customer. Tell me about the situation, the strategies you considered and how you resolved the situation."

A variation of this concept is to pick up on claims made by the candidate. In asking a candidate about strengths, that person might have said, "I was the inspirational leader of my team at my last job." You might then ask, "You say you were the inspirational leader at your last job. Give me an example of how you applied this ability. Tell me the situation, what you did, and how you knew you were inspiring others."

Stress interviews. This approach is particularly helpful in hiring for positions that involve significant stress. The applicant is asked questions and then is challenged about their answers. The interviewer might also ask the questions in rapid succession to hinder the person's ability to respond. Finally the interviewer might fake a disagreement with the candidate to see how they respond. Stress interviews should only be used in specific situations when the job involves high emotional stress.

Digi-Lectronics, Inc.

Attracting the Best Employees

Use this card with candidates for all positions. It provides facts and tips that can be used to persuade the best candidates to come work for us. While it is important to persuade people, make sure you are persuading the right people. Do not lead individuals on and be extremely careful about making commitments you or the company cannot keep.

In explaining the company to a candidate, have you mentioned that:

- We offer a close-knit atmosphere where the benefits of a small company can be used to advantage
- We offer cross training which will broaden their skills and experience.
- We have an educational opportunity program which reimburses for related course work completed with a grade of "B" or better.
- Our benefits program includes dental and eye coverage as part of the base package.
- That we are considered one of the top three manufacturers of the digital switch systems in the nation.
- That our revenues have grown a minimum of 15% each year for the past three.
- That we have a stock ownership program for all regular employees.

Test clerical skills. As the clerical world becomes increasingly complex, it is critical that you ascertain candidates' actual skills. Too many organizations have been burned by individuals claiming certain expertise, when those skills were minimal at best. A typing test, phone handling, word processing and data base management all fall into this category. Don't ask! Test!

It is imperative that new employees fit in. Suggest to final candidates that they stop by and introduce themselves to a selection of individuals with whom they would be working. Provide the names and locations, but let them go by themselves. These visits do not have to take more than five minutes each. Quick evaluations from the people they visited will give you one more impression of their probability for success.

Invite final candidates for all positions to unconventional activities. Ask them to join the company softball team for a night. Allow them to sit in on one of your weekly wrap-ups. Invite them to a Friday afternoon gathering with other employees. Ask them out to dinner and include their spouses.

While all of the above must be explained as optional, those who do participate in these opportunities will provide another glimpse at someone who could contribute to your organization intimately over the next several years.

Portraying the Company

Throughout the interview process, remember that you

Interviewing Those with Disabilities

With the enactment of the Americans with Disabilities Act of 1990, every employer must become more aware how those applicants with disabilities are treated during the interview process. Here are a few tips for making the interview process for disabled applicants more comfortable.

1. Keep the interview focused on the applicant's qualifications. Do not ask for instance, "How will you get to work?" Instead, ask job related questions such as, "How will you perform this task?"

2. Remember to shake hands and make eye contact without staring. Treat the applicant like an adult. It is okay to offer assistance, but don't be offended if it is not accepted.

3. If interviewing a wheelchair-bound applicant, do not push or grasp the chair unless the applicant asks you to do so. Move any furniture that makes it difficult for the person to maneuver. Sit in a chair that allows you to be at the applicant's eye level.

4. If the applicant is deaf, use a physical signal such as tapping the person's hand if you need to get their attention. Don't shout. If an interpreter is not present, you may have to rely on lip reading gestures and note passing. Enunciate clearly and situate yourself so that your face is easily seen.

5. When interviewing someone who is blind, identify yourself and any others present. Cue a handshaking by saying, "May we shake hands?" Then touch the person's hand. Be clear when giving directions. Say for example, "The chair is six steps to your left."

6. When speaking with someone who is mentally retarded, use simple language. Repeat any directions several times and give positive feedback when appropriate.

need to sell the company as much as each candidate needs to sell you. *The candidates you want do their homework, investigate your organization, and ask the toughest questions when their turn comes.*

You need to be prepared to answer these questions and discuss their concerns. This applies to all candidates, not just those with their eyes on the boardroom. If your assembly workers are not emotionally invested in what they're doing, they will not work as effectively.

Your process must work correctly. Is it timely? Is your staff punctual? Are they prepared? Are they excited about the prospect of adding a new member to the team?

All of this makes an impression, positive or negative. Interview applicants as if they were your best customers.

VII. The Interview Checklist

_____ 1. Do you evaluate every position fully before interviewing, to ascertain what information is needed?

_____ 2. Are you certain that all questions are job related?

_____ 3. Do you design the process to assure professionalism before proceeding with the interviews?

_____ 4. Have you developed interview report forms to handle the process?

_____ 5. Do you review candidate information, questions to be asked, and setting before every interview?

_____ 6. Do you rehearse the interview before seeing the first candidate to assure professionalism?

_____ 7. Do you limit the number of candidates you initially interview to no more than six per position?

_____ 8. Do you outline the interview for the candidate before proceeding?

_____ 9. Do you take non-verbal cues into consideration when interviewing?

_____10. Do you take notes during interviews to avoid confusion?

_____11. Do you indicate to every interviewed candidate when they can expect to hear a result?

_____12. Do you write an interview summary after every candidate?

_____13. Do you evaluate interviews after you have conducted them to improve your skills?

_____14. Have you considered the alternative interview strategies mentioned in this chapter?

_____15. Are you conscious of having to "sell" the company when interviewing candidates?

_____16. Do you conduct an evaluation of the interview process after every new hire?

Obtaining Reliable References

"Would you hire Jim again?" asked the recruiter.

"Well…yes," replied the manager.

"Are there any reasons you might be hesitant?" pressed the recruiter.

"I said I would re-hire him," the manager snapped. "Do you want to know anything else?"

"No," said the recruiter. "I think I've got all I need to know."

Here's What You'll Learn

I.   Conducting a Reference Check
II.   Checking Credentials
III.   The Reference Checklist

Other than the information on a resume or application, an employer has little with which to evaluate various applicants. While references provide data about only past performance, they may still be helpful in ascertaining the competence and value of an applicant.

Whereas traditionally references were provided in written form, most employers have turned to phone inquiries as a more efficient means for obtaining information. In a written reference, the reader is only provided with what the author thinks is important. Thus the reader is unable to draw certain conclusions for lack of information. In calling references, the evaluator has the opportunity to ask questions more directly related to job requirements and specific performances.

Remember that one characteristic of a reference check is that it takes time. Unfortunately, many positions are hired in a rush to fill an immediate vacancy. This results in overlooking some critical elements. There is a growing proliferation of resume and credential fakers in the job market. Employers must be thorough in investigating potential employees.

This is serious business. Courts have found employers culpable where an incompetent employee was at fault. The decisions have indicated that better care should have been exercised in the hiring process. Other related incidents have cost employers, large and small, millions of dollars in damages and lost revenue.

Unfortunately, employers have also become increasingly resistant to providing references on former personnel for fear of litigation. Some companies have gone so far as to provide only the name, position held and work dates of previous employees, regardless of their performance on the job.

But without information from previous employers, the evaluator is left with little more than the applicant's word on all information sought. This obviously works to the applicant's advantage, but can result in disaster for the employer.

I. Conducting a Reference Check

A reference check must be performed in a deliberate fashion. Rushing through questions with a past employer will not achieve the results you need.

Questions should be developed around what you need to know about the applicant's performance. They must be *job related!* Fishing for personal information is just inviting trouble.

The references checked should include people with whom the candidate has worked in the past three years. Character references are generally a waste of time. If applicants do not provide the names of individuals with whom they have worked directly, that should automatically arouse suspicion.

When speaking with a reference, ask if there are other individuals who worked with the applicant and if you may speak with them. Take for granted that references listed by the candidate have been prepped for this task. Contacting someone who is unsuspecting may provide candid information, positive or negative.

On occasion, you will be referred to personnel, especially if the applicant in question left the referenced company a year or more ago. Unfortunately, personnel specialists are trained to provide only job titles and dates of employment.

If this happens, be creative. Try the department again. You might get a different person who will be more cooperative. Attempt different angles and strategies. Put the person with whom you're speaking at ease. A soothing, friendly voice may catch them off-guard.

If you're having little success, ask someone else in your organization to give it a try. How the reference taker and reference giver interact with each other plays a significant role in the information obtained.

What to Ask

Examine the requirements of the position to be filled and build your questions around this information. The questions should be consistent from reference to reference, and candidate to candidate. Developing standardized sets of questions might be appropriate.

Questions asked of business and/or professional references should be related exclusively to past job performance. It is appropriate of course, to pursue clarification if something arouses your interest as long as the conversation remains in the proper domain.

A typical set of questions might be:

- "How long did Carl work for you?"
- "Did he hold other positions within the company?"
- "How would you describe his work ethic."
- "Given the opportunity, would you hire him again?"
- "What reservations should I have about hiring him?"

- "Who else within your organization would be able to comment on his performance?"
- "What were his reasons for leaving?"

How to Ask

Develop a rapport with references. If you rush into a reference check in a perfunctory way, there is little opportunity to establish a positive relationship. While you are interested in both facts and impressions, a "just the facts madam" approach will defeat your effort.

References may be reluctant to give information on a candidate if the relationship was not as positive as one would hope. Their hesitancy can be an indication of areas you might want to pursue with other references or the candidate during an interview. People carrying out reference checks should be trained to hear not only what is said but also what is meant.

One means for obtaining information or opinion through a reluctant reference is to rephrase the question:

Q: Could you describe the work habits of Dave Lee?
A: Yeah. He worked like everyone else. Got the job done.
Q: So you would describe him as a hard worker with plenty of ambition and enthusiasm for the job?
A: Well...okay...I guess so.

In the above exchange, the reference is agreeing with what the evaluator is saying. Yet what is being said is not necessarily what is meant. An astute listener should pick up the inference. If the candidate was an excellent worker, chances are the reference would have reinforced his first statement with something like, "Absolutely! Dave Lee left a void in the morale and productivity around here. I wish I had him back."

In some cases, you have to manipulate references into answering certain questions. Stick strictly to the facts. One strategy is to create the impression that the applicant has just about been offered the job, something like, "we're down to three applicants and we're looking for the best match." How references respond verbally or nonverbally to the applicant's success thus far will leave an indication of how they

Digi-Lectronics, Inc. *Telephone Reference Guide*

Hints:
Be friendly, but persistent.
Listen for what is said and also how it is said.
If the reference is reluctant, appeal to their common sense.
Ask about others who can comment on the applicant's performance.

Record the information as you conduct the reference check.
Don't wait to write it down later.

Mr./Ms._____, this is_____with Digi-Lectric.
We are considering _____ for possible employment and I would like
to ask you a few questions about his/her work history with you.

1. What dates was s/he employed with you?
2. What was_____ 's job title?
3. What were_____ 's duties?
4. How would you describe _____ 's work ethic?
5. What would you consider _____ 's strong points?
6. Given the opportunity, would you hire _____ again?
7. What kind of supervision did _____ require?
8. What was the basis of _____'s compensation?
9. What concerns should I have about hiring _____?
10. Who else there might be able to comment on his/her performance?

If you have trouble getting through:

Call before or after regular business hours, this avoids the receptionist/gatekeeper.
If you are referred to personnel, hang up and try back at a different time.
Try to build rapport with the reference giver. If you have difficulty, ask someone else to try.
If all references are hard to reach or reluctant, that might be saying something itself.

feel about that person. Another option is the indirect inquiry. You might ask, "Since this person will be going through some training once she's on board, I am wondering if you could tell where she might need the most training."

Since references might draw the conclusion that this woman already has been offered the job, they might be more open to discussing individual characteristics.

It is up to the reference checker to provide opportunities in which the reference can convey information about a questionable employee without risking litigation. (Remember, it is up to the plaintiff to prove intent in a defamation suit.)

Robert Thornton, author of *The Lexicon of Intentionally Ambiguous Recommendations* (Meadowbrook Press, 1988), has developed a humorous set of responses a reference can give to pan applicants. They include:

"In my opinion, you will be very fortunate to get this person to work for you."

"I can assure you that no person would be better for the job."

"I most enthusiastically recommend this candidate with no qualifications whatsoever."

"I would urge you to waste no time in making this candidate an offer of employment."

Appeal to Common Sense

Still another alternative for obtaining information from reluctant references is to simply appeal to their common sense. If everyone refuses to give references on former employees, the recruiting system will experience a grave loss. Employers who are careful in what they say and document performance along the way, have nothing to fear. Unfortunately, most companies are not known for their diligence in recordkeeping and therefore leave themselves at risk in giving references.

A final option is to ask candidates to sign a release that allows former employers to speak freely about the subject's performance. It is best to have an attorney review any such release prior to its use.

II. Checking Credentials

Besides checking references, verify all other credentials for authenticity. Employers continually discover applicants who have falsified facts in order to "qualify" for a job. As competition for jobs has increased, so have the deceptions.

While some applicants may start out with a simple exaggeration, others manufacture entire degree programs to satisfy requirements. Ironically, the largest number of falsifications appear to involve the Ivy League and other well known schools. While these institutions provide badly needed credibility, they are also the first ones checked in an investigation.

When checking educational credentials, ask not only if the applicant has attended, but the dates of attendance, the program or major studied and whether s/he graduated. Having a degree in social work from Stanford is not the same as having a degree in finance, but no one knows if the resume reads "Bachelor of Science, Stanford University, Graduation, 1992."

Credit Checks

In addition to educational credentials, it is also permissible for an employer to conduct a credit check. This is advisable for a position involved with the financial dealings of the company. These credit checks are regulated by the Federal Fair Credit Reporting Act as well as many states laws. Disclosure to the applicant of such a credit check is required. Failure to do so could leave the company open to civil l iability. Consult your attorney on what may be done in your locale.

Information from a credit history can provide insight into any financial difficulties the person may be having and an account of their present financial responsibilities. One might be able to draw conclusions from this information about the likelihood of this person to mishandle funds or to take other indiscreet or illegal actions. Once again, you are protecting yourself not only against in-house loss and theft, but also against actions brought by others if the employee acts on your behalf. (This doesn't prevent the action. It does however mitigate the level of risk.)

Credential Services

A final option, if you want to avoid the hassle of this altogether, is to employ a credential service. These individuals will run a thorough background check on an applicant and report back with their evaluation. In some cases, their information will have more depth since they have time to persevere and are being paid to do so. But there is a point of diminishing returns. In some cases, the amount of data provided may not be warranted and might provide information you cannot legally use during the selection process. This can include arrest records, consumer records, driving records and other information protected by privacy laws. Be judicious in the use of these organizations.

These services are located in most cities and can be found through the local personnel association or chamber of commerce. You might also check the World Wide Web. (Key words: Background check.)

III. The Reference Checklist

____ 1. Are you taking time with your reference checks and performing them in a thorough and consistent manner? Are you planning your questions ahead of time and keeping them job-related?

____2. When checking a reference, are you asking if there are others within the organization who would be willing to add their thoughts? These might be more candid.

____3. When conducting the check, are you listening to what is being said but also to what is being meant? They may not be consistent.

_____4. Are you careful to check credentials thoroughly with all institutions listed on the resume or application?

_____5. Have you considered the option of having a credit check performed on applicants, especially if they will be involved with the finances of the company?

Chapter 10

Employment Testing: Do's and Don'ts

"I feel really funny conducting these urine tests," said the manager. "To me, whether they use dope is their business as long as they don't use it on the job."

"All this witness stuff kills morale. They think we don't trust them," agreed his colleague.

"Yeah. But then there was that accident with the packing skids," piped in a third. "If Sammie had come to work in his right mind, those wouldn't have fallen over."

"But is that any reason to test everyone?" asked the first manager. "I had a kid in here the other day and I offered her a job. I told her about the test and she said it was an invasion of privacy."

Here's What You'll Learn

I. Overview of Testing Issues

Pre-employment testing has been, and will continue to be, a controversial issue. While testing has become a valid method for ascertaining a candidate's suitability for employment, legal implications including invasion of privacy and discrimination still surround the topic.

Pre-employment screening can be divided into two categories.

Psychological screening to determine levels of skill-based competence, honesty, and mental attitudes toward performance.

Physical screening to determine fitness to perform the job. This includes drug and alcohol screening, and genetic screening.

With the exception of the transportation industry, the decision to screen, whether psychologically or physically, is totally up to the individual employer. Surveys show that the business community as a whole is divided on the issue. While testing has proven to be an accurate indicator in certain situations, it is also expensive and time consuming. Further, it opens the door to litigation if not closely monitored.

It should be assumed that little information in any organization will remain truly confidential. Therefore, the confidential results of testing, whether for honesty or physical capabilities, should be guarded closely.

Testing can be used as a recruiting device if handled correctly. Hawaiian Electric Company advertised that they would conduct testing for positions now and in the future in their organization. These applicants, having passed the test, are now eligible for positions as they come open. Because of it's good name within the community Hawaiian Electric was able to attract well over 4000 applicants who took the test and are now eligible for employment.

Requiring a physician's examination, regardless of whether you are screening for drugs, is sound advice. Some applicants suffer from pre-existing conditions such as back and head injury, due to previous accidents on or off the job. Few companies can afford to absorb the additional costs of caring for an employee who walked in the door with a pre-existing ailment. Have your company physician examine all new employees. The cost of exams should not be a consideration since the long-term effects of not doing so can be devastating. All job offers should be made with the contingency that the candidate passes the physical.

This chapter will cover five areas where testing has been implemented in the pre-employment process. Each section provides information on the purpose and use of the tests along with a discussion of the arguments surrounding their value. It closes with recommendations on the issue.

II. Paper and Pencil Testing

So-called paper and pencil testing may be divided into two categories:

- Written honesty and personality tests
- Skills and aptitude testing.

The honesty and personality tests are used to determine an applicant's tendency toward honesty and psychological indicators of how they will perform on the job. These characteristics can include truthfulness, tendency toward depression, hysteria, anger, etc.

Skills and aptitude testing on the other hand, is used to assess the candidate's ability to perform required tasks. These might include typing and mathematical skills, along with verbal and written communication.

The main controversy over paper and pencil tests is accuracy. Applicants who answer "too honestly" may be disqualified while less honest applicants who manipulate the test may be accepted.

Applicants who do not generally "test well" may do poorly on an examination even though they have the required skills or aptitudes. Tests that fail a higher than normal number of individuals in protected classes have an adverse impact and are considered to be discriminatory.

Finally, opponents to pre-employment testing maintain that it violates an individual's right to privacy. These critics point to the employers' less intrusive means for gathering information such as the interview, resume, application and reference checks.

In 1990, the U.S. Office of Technology Assessment concluded that existing research does not clearly confirm or refute the fact that paper and pencil integrity testing accurately predicts dishonest behavior in the work place. While firms producing these products refute these findings, the report still calls into question the overall validity of integrity testing.

Written Honesty and Personality Testing

With the passage of the Employee Polygraph Protection Act of 1988 (EPPA), an increasing number of employers have turned to these tests for the screening of applicants. Their major aim is to establish an applicant's propensity to be honest. It is difficult to assess an applicant's tendency toward telling the truth, but research indicates some strong correlations between those candidates considered "high risk" and those who were found likely to steal on the job.

These examinations are generally a series of multiple choice, true/false or yes/no based questions or a combination thereof. These packages come with an examination booklet and answer sheets and can be scored quickly by the employer or test vendor. They range in price from $5–14.

Most of these screening devices are now available in computerized form. In some cases, the applicant can call a toll-free number and complete the process using a touch tone telephone. In others, the testing vendor supplies software that is loaded into the employer's computer. Usage is tracked by computer and fees are assessed based on the number of applicants tested.

Some of these tests contain questions to measure the applicant's truthfulness while taking the test. These questions are interspersed throughout and ask about emotions such as "Sometimes I get frustrated on the job." Since it can be easily assumed that everyone experiences frustration, an applicant who answers "false" would automatically be suspect. This series of questions is tallied during scoring and a "lie scale" is established to reference how truthful the applicant is being.

Skills and Aptitude Testing

Employers must be careful in the use of skills and aptitude testing. As indicated above, the possibility of adverse impact, and therefore discrimination, exists unless the results of these tests are closely monitored.

Honesty and personality testing generally consists of standardized instruments. Skill and aptitude tests on the other hand, may be published examinations such as the Wonderlic Personnel Test which attempts to measure verbal intelligence, or tests created by the employer to assess capabilities in a certain area. The latter group includes physical measures such as coordination and lifting as well as tests of typing, letter writing, and organization of paperwork.

Some testing has become rather creative. Japanese automobile firms for instance employ assessment centers involving in-basket exercises and production line testing including team games requiring applicants to assemble a certain number of flashlights in a given period of time. The purpose behind these tests is to discover who may fit in which position the best.

Dependability Testing

Dependability tests are used to forecast an applicant's likelihood for success on the job. These tests are an adaptation of what industrial psychologists have termed trait testing. This variation on trait testing evaluates an applicant's attitudes, practices and values that are job related as compared to a so-called cognitive test which attempts to measure reasoning and learning.

A dependability test that is designed for a company is validated to show that there is a clear relationship between a particular test result and job performance. These tests vary from an integrity test in that they evaluate a variety of values instead of honesty alone. Developers of dependability tests maintain that integrity tests will do little more than predict how applicants will do on a polygraph examination.

Each company must score its own tests since the test is developed specifically for that organization. Some have a pass/fail cut-off and others have a system allowing for a range of scores. Subjective judgments and other factors are usually incorporated into the hiring process as well. Developers' experiences to date have shown that these tests work best with businesses that have many employees and experience a high turnover rate of non-management personnel.

The cost of developing these tests is generally $20–30,000. But each company owns the test developed for it and the cost of each administration declines with use. For a firm with about 3000 employees for example, the average cost of the test can be approximately 30 cents per applicant.

Validation

The Equal Employment Opportunity Commission (EEOC) allows employers to use skill and aptitude testing as a form of pre-employment selection. Employers should be aware however, that the validity of using a test in one circumstance does not guarantee that it may be used in another.

The EEOC does not require that these tests be validated unless it can be shown that they produce an adverse impact. In other words, an employer can use any test s/he wishes, but must be able to prove, if challenged, that the test does not discriminate against protected classes.

To assure that the testing has no adverse effect, most employers "validate" their tests through one of three methods approved by the commission:

- content validity studies
- criterion validity studies
- construct validity studies

Content validity studies establish that the content of the test is consistent with the duties and responsibilities of the job. A test, for instance, that questions an applicant's ability to perform basic mathematics for a bank teller's position has content validity.

Criterion validity studies measure the predictability of the test-taker to succeed on the job. If there is a significant statistical correlation between the test results and subject's performance on the job, then the test is considered valid.

Construct validity studies are the least used of the three because of their complex nature. These studies measure the evidence of the effect to which a subject's individual characteristics match identifiable characteristics of the job. Because of the amount of empirical data required to establish validity, these studies have been declared invalid numerous times.

The most convincing proof that a test is valid is found in a predictive validity study. This is a study in which the test is administered to job applicants, their attitudes recorded, and their behavior on the job is tracked. When deciding which test to use, consider practical testing features such as the test's required reading level, ease of administration, computer scoring technology, ease of scoring, clarity of test output, pass rate, satisfied client references and the test's business history. Finally evaluate the test publisher's ability to provide thorough training to your test administrators.

Handwriting Analysis

Another means for assessing individuals is through analysis of their handwriting. While this method has been popular in Europe for years, it is relatively new to our employment system.

Handwriting analysis involves a review of the physical characteristics of a person's handwriting such as size and slant of the letters, pressure on the paper and the rhythm with which the writing was produced. In some cases, handwriting analysis can provide selection officials with a new perspective on job candidates who otherwise might be overlooked because of difficulty with another part of the selection process.

A number of employers have expressed a high degree of satisfaction with the results of handwriting analysis. They claim it is a simpler and less expensive system to administer than psychological tests.

While some companies have given this technique high ratings, critics charge that there is no scientific basis for the conclusions drawn. Analysis of this type range from $25-$400 per person.

Recommendations for Paper and Pencil Testing

Know why you are testing. What information do you expect a paper and pencil test to provide that will assist you in hiring more accurately?

Consider the impact of employee testing on employee morale. Trust is a delicate balance in any organization. Many employees view testing as a statement of distrust. Consult with employees about problems related to theft. They might have a better solution.

Check state regulations on pre-employment testing in addition to federal statutes. In many cases, these requirements are more stringent or totally prohibit certain forms of testing.

When using pre-employment testing, make sure it is not having an adverse impact on protected classes of applicants. Recordkeeping is essential in addition to confidentiality.

Examine the cost/benefit ratio of using tests in the pre-employment process. While these instruments can provide an indication of a person's honesty and capabilities, the annual expense for this information might better be used elsewhere.

Check references and reputations of testing services and products.

Be sure the test is measuring what you want it to measure. Researching a test before using it is critical. Will it give you the information you seek? Look past the fancy product packaging.

Be sure all testing is validated. All instruments, published and employer created, should be checked for relatedness to the job duties. This needs to be done for each type of position. There is no such thing as a blanket test.

If you have created your own tests for certain positions, have them validated by an outside source following the Guidelines for Employee Selection Procedures available from the Equal Employment Opportunity Commission.

III. Selecting Integrity Tests

Employee theft has become a national problem. According to the National Business Crime Information Network, American businesses lose more than $200 billion every year to cash and merchandise thefts committed by employees. The Department of Justice has estimated that insider theft is growing at 15 percent annually.

One option is administering integrity tests to all those you plan to hire. Paper-and-pencil integrity testing has been in use for more than fifty years and has evolved into a multi-million dollar industry. Firms such as Reid Psychological Systems, Stanton Corporation and McGraw-London House, Inc. have developed a host of honesty tests that can be taken in five to thirty minutes and claim to reveal whether the applicant is likely to steal or otherwise act dishonestly on the job.

A debate about the reliability of these tests has raged for years and no clear answer is in sight. Many of the firms who use them swear by their accuracy. They maintain that since polygraph testing is no longer an option, these tests provide a reasonable alternative. They argue that if administered properly and tracked closely, these tests will provide a reliable predictor of applicant honesty. Yet in a 1990 survey by the American Management Association only 6.2% of businesses responding indicated that they use integrity tests as part of their applicant screening process.

If you do decide to investigate the testing option, here are seven quick tips for making the job effective:

Know why you are testing. What is being stolen? Is it concentrated in one department? Does one site have more theft than others? What other options for reducing theft might you have? What information do you expect an integrity test to provide that will help you hire more accurately? Have plenty of questions for every testing firm you approach.

Consider the impact of testing on employee morale. Trust in any organization is a delicate balance. Many employees view integrity testing as a statement of distrust. Consult with employees about problems related to theft. Ask for their input since company losses have an effect on everyone. Their active participation in theft prevention might have more of an impact than any integrity test.

Check federal, state and local regulations for testing prohibitions. Before approaching testing firms, consult with your attorney about state and local laws regarding pre-employment testing.

Be sure the test is validated. While there are no federal laws banning tests, the test you give must fall within the validity guidelines of the Equal Employment Opportunity Commission. These guidelines assure that the test is measuring what it is supposed to measure reliably.

Make sure the test is not going to have an adverse impact on those groups from which you hire. In addition to being reliable, the test should not discriminate against protected classes of people.

Thoroughly check the references of the testing firm you plan use. Ask for the names and contacts of at least three other comparable firms who are using the test with success. Then ask lots of questions, especially around the test's reliability in distinguishing between honest and dishonest applicants.

Finally, recognize that there is no such thing as the perfect test. While everyone has a desire to have a "black and white" answer about applicant honesty, these tests no matter how reliable are only one part of the equation in hiring honest people for the job.

IV. Polygraph Screening

The purpose of the polygraph or lie-detector is to determine whether an applicant is telling the truth. Proponents claim that on this basis it can be projected whether a candidate will be honest on the job.

One of the major pieces of federal legislation passed in 1988 was the Employee Polygraph Protection Act. Having taken effect December 27, 1988, it effectively prohibits private sector use of polygraphs, voice print devices and related technology for screening applicants. There are exceptions to this, but they are limited to certain jobs involving defense and national security, pharmaceuticals and private security firms.

Overall Considerations

The polygraph has been the source of controversy for a number of years. As with other forms of testing, the major issue is accuracy.

The basic logic behind the polygraph is that lying creates stress and that this stress can be measured mechanically. This mechanically measured stress can then be used to determine whether the candidate tends to be dishonest based on whether s/he lied during the examination.

The most common form of polygraph testing is the Relevant Control Method, where the subject is asked a series of questions, some related to the job and others irrelevant. Applicants might be asked, for instance, if they have ever shopped for groceries. The stress associated with the answer will be recorded mechanically. When asked if they have ever stolen anything from an employer, the stress related to this answer will also be recorded. The levels of stress recorded for both should be relatively the same. If the stress is significantly higher on the question regarding theft, it is concluded that the subject is lying.

But there are ways to manipulate the test. Use of muscle tension, drugs, or physical stress such as pinching oneself can alter the outcome of data.

The location in which a test is taken may also be a factor along with the training of the polygraph operator. Finally, honest subjects who are nervous about taking the test may fail because of apprehension. Error rates in the polygraph have been estimated as high as 50%.

Legal Ramifications

Practically speaking, it is not wise to even contemplate the use of a polygraph in your business. While employers are still allowed to use this equipment to investigate theft and employee misconduct, the guidelines are so complicated that it could prove more of a harm than a help.

Recommendations

If you are eligible to administer polygraph tests, be extremely careful in your interpretation of the guidelines. The act is enforced by the Wage and Hour Division of the Department of Labor. Check any procedures with them before proceeding. If you are a defense contractor, check to make sure use of the polygraph is necessary under your agreement.

If you do choose to use this technology, here are a few recommendations:

Make sure the purpose falls within the guidelines of the EPPA. Simple lack of trust is not an acceptable reason for administering the polygraph. You must be able to defend your use in court.

Select your polygraph examiner carefully. Ask for references. In states where a license or certification is required, ask to see it. The examining firm should be a member of the American Polygraph Association. Ask if they have ever been named as defendants in a lawsuit concerning their polygraph examinations?

Know exactly what you're testing for. Review with the examiner what questions will be asked and have your attorney check these questions for acceptability. Polygraph examiners are considered agents of the employer.

Acknowledgment of Polygraph Testing

I acknowledge that Digi-Lectronics, Inc. will be administering polygraph examinations to employees whenever the company believes that such an examination is warranted. I understand that the company will make every effort to schedule such an examination at a mutually agreeable time and that refusal to submit to a polygraph examination is grounds for termination of employment.

Employers: *This type of clause is included in the application forms of companies where security is extremely important. With few exceptions, federal law now prohibits the use of polygraphs in the screening of applicants. Be sure to check federal regulations before administering such a test.* *

Be honest with all applicants. If applicants will be rejected after failing the polygraph, tell them. Leading them on with promises of possible exceptions can only damage your selection process and leave you open to litigation.

Have all applicants sign a consent form. This procedure eliminates claims that the polygraph was conducted under duress or that permission was never given.

Keep all records absolutely confidential. Under no circumstances should anyone have access to these files unless authorized to do so.

Consider the "second chance." It is very possible for some honest individuals to fail the polygraph for the reasons given above. If there is a reasonable doubt always give the applicant the opportunity to take the polygraph a second time to verify results.

Much has been written on the subject of polygraph screening. See the bibliography for additional sources.

V. Genetic Screening

On the horizon of pre-employment testing is the area of genetic screening. While the courts have made no definitive statements regarding its use, you should be familiar with its purposes and procedures. Employers using any chemicals within the work place on a large scale basis should pay special attention to this information.

Genetic screening involves testing for certain human characteristics most commonly through blood samples. With the proliferation of chemicals that have entered the work place in the past 50 years, scientists are discovering that certain individuals react differently to certain substances than others, due to these characteristics. In some cases, these reactions can be harmful. The purpose of genetic screening is to ascertain whether an applicant will experience an adverse reaction to chemicals found within a work place. The Toxic Substances Act requires all employers to post notice of any toxic chemicals or compounds being used on the premises.

The Arguments

Genetic screening was introduced with the best of intentions. Employers using certain substances within the work place became concerned with the possible side effects employees were having to these compounds. In an effort to maintain a safe work environment, they began testing employees and applicants to determine why such reactions were taking place. Out of this sprung a practice of screening all employees. While opponents of genetic screening acknowledge the good intentions, they also raise concerns about these issues:

- Because certain races are more likely to contain certain genetic characteristics, is this another way to block the hiring of these groups?
- If certain chemicals react dangerously when in contact with employees, why are they being used in the work place? If they are a necessity, why isn't there more care taken with their handling?

Little has been done at this time to answer these concerns. The United States Office of Technology Assessment, while studying the subject extensively, has not approved any of the screening technology for routine use in the work place. At the same time, it has not been prohibited.

Opponents have argued that discrimination by genetic characteristics falls under Title VII of the Civil Rights Act of 1964. But according to this legislation, genetic characteristics are not a protected class.

Finally, the Occupational Safety and Health Administration makes no mention of genetic screening in the work place. However, this legislation does mandate that in a pre-employment physical examination, the physician must take into consideration a wide range of physical conditions.

What does this mean for the employer? While this is not a large issue at the present time, attention to it could have an impact on organizations using any of the 35,000 chemicals currently in use in business. This situation could range from toner in the photocopier on one extreme to hazardous toxins on the other. The bottom line is to remain informed.

Recommendations

Perform a thorough analysis of your work place if considering genetic screening. This situation will not apply to most companies. If you are considering this type of selection, be extremely aware of its ramifications.

Genetic screening if implemented, should be part of an overall physical. It should not be used simply to reject applicants. If certain traits are revealed, you might consider offering the applicant less hazardous placement within the firm.

Take care in selecting the testing service. As with other testing services, referrals and reliable information should be sought to establish credibility.

VI. Drug and Alcohol Screening

With the proliferation of drug and alcohol abuse in the United States, worker productivity has been increasingly affected. Impaired employees can also present a safety hazard within the work environment. With the advance in technology and the addition of thousands of dangerous chemicals and machines to the work place, attentiveness is mandatory at all times.

With companies becoming more cost conscious, each person's attendance and productivity have a greater impact. If your only lathe operator is absent, a number of employees might have to adjust their schedules and tasks. A missing receptionist can play havoc with the phones. Each person is critical and if drugs are a problem, the normal flow of daily work can be disrupted.

The Controversy

As with any controversy, there are legitimate arguments on both sides. Regardless of your feelings toward the use and abuse of these products, you have a responsibility as an employer to provide a safe, profitable work place while still staying within the law.

Proponents of testing for drugs point out that the work place becomes safer when testing is performed and therefore demonstrates the employer's concern for the health and well-being of the employees. In addition, the rate of productivity rises which has a positive effect on morale. If applicants know that when they apply for a job they will be screened for drugs, you may well save substantial money simply because they will not apply and be tested. They add that many of the drugs are controlled substances and therefore employees possessing them are breaking the law.

Critics of testing for drugs maintain that potential employees' rights to privacy are being violated since what the applicants do on their own time is their business. Secondly, they complain about the poor levels of accuracy for many of the testing techniques, in some cases as high as 50%. Many false positives are also reported because of medication the applicant may be taking at the time.

Additionally, opponents maintain that abusers who have completed a treatment program are considered disabled under the Americans with Disabilities Act. Current abusers could be classified as handicapped under the Rehabilitation Act of 1973 and are a protected class. This second law covers employers with federal contracts and/or funding.

Finally, critics point out that the testing could have a disparate impact on protected classes under Title VII of the Civil Rights Act of 1964. This means, for instance, that certain groups, where a higher incidence of abuse has been established will be faced with discrimination.

General worker attitudes may also have an influence on drug testing. Seventy percent of the 1000 workers polled by the Gallup Organization said that employers should have the right to test employees suspected of drug use. More that 50 percent supported random drug testing.

The Legalities of Testing

At this point, the federal government has not acted directly to regulate drug and alcohol testing in the work place. As mentioned above, the Rehabilitation Act of 1973 might be used by some applicants to avoid the testing issue. This could be done only if applicants are willing to admit that they have abused the substance and then claim the handicap. Most are not willing to do so. The law has been interpreted to mean that. an employer can only refuse to hire when the handicap of alcoholism or drug addiction would make the applicant unable or unqualified to perform in the position.

Another consideration would be disparate impact under the Civil Rights Act of 1964. Currently however, there have been no federal court decisions regarding this particular issue.

Finally, the National Labor Relations Board has taken the position that testing for drugs should be a mandatory subject of collective bargaining and that these negotiations should take place prior to the implementation of a program.

Legal Considerations of Drug Screening

- There are no federal guidelines regulating drug screening.

- Applicants who have abused drugs in the past are considered disabled under the Americans with Disabilities Act provided they completed or are in the process of completing a treatment program. Those currently abusing drugs are not protected.

- Applicants may invoke the Rehabilitation Act of 1973 if:
  1. The employer is within the Act's jurisdiction.
  2. The applicant is willing to admit to drug abuse.

- Employers within the jurisdiction of Title VII may risk a disparate impact.

- While pre-screening applicants for drugs has become a generally accepted practice, random screening of current employees is still being debated due to privacy considerations.

- Unionized employers should assume that drug screening will be a part of the collective bargaining agreement.

- No state has specifically prohibited drug screening. Applicants' rights of privacy is a current issue.

On the state level, some action has been taken to address applicants' rights of privacy concerning alcohol and drug testing. While no state has passed legislation specifically prohibiting drug testing, Alaska and California have specific privacy guarantees covering private employment.

Procedures for Testing

While it is not the author's intent to provide a full scale explanation of drug testing, familiarity with the concepts is helpful.

Most employers who are currently screening for substance abuse use a urine testing procedure. There are other more sophisticated methods available involving blood, breath, skin, hair, and saliva.

The most common test used by laboratories providing these services is "enzyme multiplied immunoassay" which measures the reaction of the urine specimen to radioactive animal antibodies. This reaction indicates the presence of drugs. The "gas chromatography mass spectrometry" (GC-MS) test is considered the most accurate and is used to confirm the presence of drugs since the initial screening has a higher error rate.

Confirming screenings should always be performed. Tests can produce a "false positive" reaction because some bodily chemicals may be detected as illegal drugs. Some over-the-counter pain relievers and prescription drugs produce the same effect.

In the course of a drug screening, other legitimate drugs the applicant is using will be identified. These however, may indicate conditions of an emotional or physical nature such as depression or epilepsy. You should be careful to judge applicants on the hiring criteria for the job, not on your emotional reaction to one of the conditions. Some may also be protected under disability legislation.

If you have chosen to implement a screening program, selection of a laboratory service is critical. Check references thoroughly. Ask to see facilities and what procedures are used. Ask why the laboratory considers its testing methods to be accurate.

Your organization should execute an agreement with the laboratory re-emphasizing the importance of confidentiality that includes a "hold harmless" clause making the *laboratory,* not the company, liable for negligence in the event of litigation. A "chain of custody" should be established for every specimen to assure proper handling. A careful record should be kept, tracing the location of each specimen at all times. This discourages tampering and the switching of samples.

Any applicant who does test positively should be given the opportunity for a confirming test to assure accuracy, even if this is at the applicant's expense.

Recommendations

Be careful to define why screening for alcohol and drugs is important to your organization. Don't be caught in the periodic waves of publicity surrounding this topic. Testing can be much more trouble than its worth.

Drug screenings should be conducted as part of an overall physical, not as an isolated pre-employment criterion. The appearance of a "witch-hunt" will attract litigation. These tests should be conducted out of a genuine concern for the organization and the applicant.

Investigate laboratories thoroughly before proceeding. Check references, methods, accuracy, and "chain of custody."

Have applicants sign a release, if at all possible, before conducting a screening for substance abuse. Make sure the applicants understand that their refusal means automatic elimination from consideration.

Test only those who have been offered a position. Make the offer contingent upon the person passing the necessary tests. This eliminates potential discrimination liability and additional costs.

Applicants who fail the drug screening should be rejected on the basis of their not passing the physical. This should eliminate difficult questions and explanations.

Maintain absolute confidentiality at all times. All records should be locked and marked confidential. Only "need-to-know" personnel should know the results.

VII. Performance Based Testing

An alternative to drug screening is that of performance based testing. While generally administered to current employees, it warrants mention in this chapter. This type of testing requires employees on a daily basis to pass a test demonstrating various abilities required for performance on the job. These might include visual acuity, hand/eye coordination, reflex timing and other elements of physical fitness. The technology generally involves a computer based-video game requiring employees to pass a test before going on the job.

Companies using this presently include trucking firms, taxis and entertainment/tour companies requiring professional drivers. The applications for this are wide spread and certainly provide a viable alternative to drug screening.

Performance testing measures *current impairment* from a variety of sources including drugs, alcohol, fatigue, stress, and emotion. Testing for current impairment provides the employers with an evaluation of the employee's actual physical and mental state at the time of work. Drug testing requires a significant waiting time for results. Performance based testing can also be performed every day without raising questions of privacy. After the original investment. it generally cost less than one dollar per employee, per working day.

Because it measures impairment rather than presence of drugs, performance based testing enables employers to screen workers every-day, better ensuring that drugs and alcohol are not impairing their performance.

Drug use may not be the only reason employees fail these tests. Employees who have experienced a traumatic experience, such as an auto accident, prior to arriving at work may show impairment during the test.

If a person being tested cannot reach a level of proficiency previously established, then the employer can surmise that something is wrong and take appropriate action. As performance testing catches on, it will provide an extremely viable alternative to the controversy surrounding drug screening.

Recommendations

Determine what you wish to measure with a performance based test. What constitutes adequate performance for each position being tested?

Thoroughly research the various alternatives for performance based testing. These would include video games, physical performance exercises such as lifting and manual coordination.

Research federal state and local regulations to assure compliance with law.

Determine start-up costs. These may be significant at first and diminish with long term use of the equipment. Costs include, video hardware, software development and training time. Some firms have found that insurance companies are willing to subsidize these costs due to eventually savings in accident prevention.

IX. The Testing Checklist

_____1. If you are considering the use of pre-employment testing, have you fully investigated the effectiveness of these tests, the legal liabilities involved and the costs per applicant?

_____2. Have you checked your paper and pencil test for validity as outlined in the federal Guidelines for Employee Selection Procedures?

_____3. If you are considering the use of a polygraph, have you checked federal regulations to be sure your use is permitted?

_____4. If you are screening for genetic factors, have you investigated all considerations involved such as legal liabilities, procedures, laboratories, and costs?

_____5. If you are screening for drugs and alcohol, have you considered all aspects of legal liability, procedures, alternatives and costs involved?

Landing Performers: Making the Right Offer

"I am making the decision," said the owner as he walked out of the room. "And my decision is Romano. I have seen all the candidates and I know you all like different people. But my choice is the one that stands."

"Why did he ask us to participate if he had already chosen Romano?" complained the marketing manager. "I was shocked when she made it through the first round."

"I can see what you're saying," agreed the controller. "Weaver's always been my top candidate because of his track record."

"Yeah, but we let Weaver slip through our fingers because our leader didn't act in time."

Here's What You'll Learn

I. Final Selection
II. Notifying Candidates
III. Negotiating Offers and Compensation
IV. The Decision-making Checklist

Although it may appear simple on the surface, selection of the final candidate is a difficult task. There are many factors to be considered. Does this person really have the qualifications? Will they fit in? Will they get the job done? Can the organization meet the compensation expectations?

I. Final Selection

Selecting and luring candidates has become much more complicated than in the past. There are many factors considered surrounding applicants' wishes for life balance, compensation, and challenging work environment. Where once making an offer almost guaranteed the person would come to work with your firm, most organizations now have to be more cognizant of selling the candidate on why s/he should work for the company.

In a tight job market, good candidates are in more demand. Therefore selection needs to be timely. Following through on promises for decision making are of paramount importance. Hiring candidates who will remain for a long tenure is critical to hiring success. Writer and consultant, Harvey MacKay observes that his "acid test" for hiring is to ask yourself, "How would you feel having this person working for the competition?"

The mechanics of final selection should be approached methodically. The number of people involved should be limited to only those necessary. Attempting to reach consensus, unless there is only one truly outstanding candidate, is time-consuming and counterproductive. For labor and clerical positions one decision-maker is optimal. This person should be the position's immediate supervisor since s/he will have the best working knowledge of job requirements and environment.

For managerial levels, a maximum of three should be involved. These individuals should include the immediate supervisor, and perhaps two managers from other departments with which the person will have contact. On occasion, it might be a good idea for final candidates to meet with the president and other executives. This assures support for the hire. Meeting with the executive staff also tends to impress and lure a particularly strong candidate.

A Logical Sequence

The selection process must follow a logical sequence. Applicant pools should be narrowed, based on a previously developed list of criteria.

Records should be kept concerning the reasons why some candidates were passed on when others weren't. These records are not only necessary for organization of the process, but also to protect the company. If a rejected applicant files suit you may be formally requested to justify your reasons for refusing that particular person.

It is best to develop a form such as the ones below to assess various criteria and qualifications. All questions on this form should be job-related. These can include qualifications, evaluation of skills and experience, along with education and training. It is extremely important to remind interviewers that comments made on these forms should be *job-related.* Biased remarks, certain attitudinal evaluations, even doodles may be interpreted as discriminatory if examined later.

When filling a position look at the candidates' desire to learn new skills. Filling a position with a candidate who meets 80% of the job requirements allows that individual to grow. Filling the position with someone who is totally qualified may result in premature turnover due to lack of challenge.

In making final the final selection, there are two options available. One is to compare candidate against candidate. The second is to match each candidate against a common standard, namely the job description. Valid arguments can be made for both practices.

Some maintain that comparing candidates to each other is a more reasonable means for judging available talent since matching them against a standard might very well be unrealistic. Who we have pictured as the perfect candidate does not always exist in real life. This reasoning does not infer you have to compromise. It does mean however, that your final candidates are probably a good representation of who can fill the position.

Others maintain that comparing candidates can lower the standards originally defined. If none of the candidates meet the standards, are you still going to choose the "best" candidate even though that person does not match the defined characteristics?

These individuals maintain that it is better to reject all candidates and begin the search again. While this is time-consuming, settling for an inferior choice is counterproductive. Before proceeding with a new search however, review your recruiting and selection techniques to make sure the system is not at fault.

Obviously, there is no correct answer to the dilemma. Consider your timing of need, importance of the position, complexity of duties and normal turnover in deciding which practice to use.

Competing for the Best

As the competition for skilled employees grows, you will need more effective strategies for securing the people you want. But landing skilled employees is not the only concern. Hiring lower skilled, enthusiastic workers has become a major concern in many firms, especially due to the high cost of replacement. Where in the past, you may have been accustomed to taking your time in the recruiting process, you now need to move more quickly to sell to your targeted applicants before they take a job with the competition.

Romancing the top candidate should begin immediately after the initial screening of resumes. Anticipating his or her concerns will enable you to treat them with care, helping them to develop a positive perception of your organization. Will the little extra touches may be time consuming, they will be more than valuable in hiring a top candidate with a long tenure.

Here are a few hints to get the job done:

Keep the knowledge of who is being interviewed on a need-to-know basis. Every organization has gossips. Ask candidates if they are aware of anyone who has joined your company recently from their company. Take steps to avoid embarrassing meetings in the hall or word getting back to their current employer.

Share as much information as you can with your strongest applicants. The top people will appreciate the opportunity to get to know your company in depth.

Escort candidates from interview to interview. This little touch keeps everyone on track and gives the opportunity for a little informal chatting between session.

Have a substitute ready for each scheduled interviewer. This eliminates delays and disruptions in the selection process. (Be sure to weed out all people who do not sell the company is its best light.)

Recognize that this is a negotiating process. Plan for all contingencies before entering into discussions. Consider all factors including salary, benefits, working conditions, location, independence and so on.

Establish a common language. Ask for clarification of each applicant's needs, desires, and qualities. Misunderstandings can be costly later on.

Look for "hot buttons" during your conversation with the top candidates that will reveal what the person's real priorities are and the their about the job. Clues to this would be comments about success, needs for recognition or monetary reward or challenge. A penetrating sample questions would be "What things are important to you in your career development?

Use your intuition. If something doesn't feel right, investigate. Sometimes uncomfortable facts have to be uncovered. But better now than later.

Don't be afraid to sell. Applicants, especially those in high demand areas need to be wooed. Ask them directly, "What will it take for you to come to work for us?" Get them to identify all concerns and desires. Then go about addressing each one to mutual satisfaction.

Act quickly. Deliberating for too long a time, will result in missed opportunities.

Involve as few people in the process as possible. Even for an executive level position, the maximum number of decision makers should be three.

Conduct the hiring process as if you are beginning a new working relationship with an applicant. This gets your strong candidates invested from the start.

Candidate Selection Form #1

Position_____
Supervisor_____
Date of Selection_____

Applicants

Priority Rating
1 = Low 5 = Critical

Applicant Rating
1 = Does not meet requirement
5 = Exceeds expectations

Priority	Required Qualifications

Priority	Preferred Characteristics

Priority of Choice	

Limit your finalists to three at the most. Spreading your energy between too many candidates dilutes the emphasis on each one. They need to feel special!

Get on their wave length. Conduct the interviews in a conversational style. Do what you can to give them special attention. Remember you're attempting to answer their needs as well as yours.

Striving to Be the Preferred Employer

As our culture's priorities change, employers must be more aware of how to attract the nest candidates. Priorities such as balance of life, challenging work are becoming more important than actual income and job security. What you are doing, as an employer, to foster a work environment that addresses these needs and yet provide workers with a balance of life outside the job.

Candidate Selection Form #2

Name of applicant_____
Address_____
Applying for _____ Phone_____
Interviewer_____ Date _____

Write required and desired qualifications in order of priority in the spaces provided. Place your ratings for this candidate in the categories indicated. (Rating: 1 = Unacceptable,   5 = Exceeds expectations)

Qualifications required	Rating
Total Score =	

Qualifications desired	Rating
Total Score =	

Companies on the forefront of employee satisfaction, make personal and family matters an integral part of the work place. They provide scheduling options such as flex-time to enable those with children to provide better child care. They provide on-site or contract child care facilities.

These companies pay more attention to specific groups and their needs. They pay attention to the needs of retirees and single mothers. They address the scheduling needs of students enrolled in classes.

As these issues and target groups are addressed, each group develops a better perception of the company they are working for. This results in lower turnover, better productivity, and a stimulating work environment. Perks that have been provided include on site fitness facilities, centers for leadership and management development, opportunities to take elder care or child care leave and housing assistance in areas of the country where the cost of living is exorbitant.

Regardless of who you hire and at what level, your organization's ability to attract the best, will become more and more dependent on your ability to be perceived as a preferred employer.

Don't Misrepresent the Company

Promising what you can't deliver results in premature turnover. Trust is the most important element of an employment relationship. While you want to put your best foot forward, you should also be up front about the working conditions, politics, policies, company growth and health. Throwing prospective employees a curve ball will only serve to make them distrustful once they are on board.

For many candidates, hours of work and possibilities for advancement are big issues. A candidate who is told one thing about these issues and then discovers another, will be more likely to leave resulting in thousands of dollars of replacement cost. Misrepresentation may also lead to a poor reputation in the community, making it difficult if not impossible to reach quality applicants.

Smaller employers may have to overcome candidates' apprehension about working in riskier situations. Rather than avoiding the issue, address the concern up front using the best possible terms. The same strategy holds true in organizations that are experiencing a downturn in business or bad publicity at the time they are hiring. Be prepared to answer questions about information or hearsay the candidates may have heard in the media.

Make your top candidates understand the working conditions within your organization. This is especially relevant if your company requires heavy or dirty or physical work. Some forms have resorted to developing a video tape of the work environment. While this may scare some individuals away, that is still better than increasing turnover. If you are interviewing on site, a plant tour serves the same purpose.

Protecting against Personal Bias

Unfortunately, it is impossible to remain totally unbiased when considering candidates for employment. The culture in which we have grown up has tempered us with a host of stereotypes and prejudices.

Do not be swayed by appearance or a pleasant personality. Resist the temptation to be overly impressed by education, training or the institution attended. Having knowledge and being able to use it are two different things.

If you identify with a candidate because of similar backgrounds, try not to allow this to influence your decision. Peculiar mannerisms can also be a distraction. Unless these would have an influence on the person's ability to perform the job, they should not be taken into consideration.

Others who try to sway your decision may also be a consideration. What are their motives? What do they get out of it? Rely on facts only and avoid rumors and innuendo.

II. Notifying Candidates

Timing is an important part of the final selection process. Just as much as you are evaluating them, they are evaluating you. While you are considering a number of applicants, they are considering a number of companies.

Swift decision-making reduces the loss of excellent candidates and also sends a clear message of corporate decisiveness. The company who waits for an "even better" candidate to come along, will probably lose their best choice to a competitor.

The entire selection process for any candidate should take no more than three weeks. Once the procedures are in place and the applications received, those doing the hiring should move along with definiteness of purpose.

An excellent way to keep everyone on target is to announce selection schedules to those candidates invited for interviews: "We will be making our second round decisions by Friday of next week. The final offer will be made three days hence." Committing yourself to this kind of plan keeps everyone motivated and satisfies the applicants' impatience.

A second means for accomplishing this is to sell those involved with the search on how acting swiftly will save them time and increase productivity: "The faster we get someone on board, the sooner we can get on with new projects."

How to Notify Candidates

Every step in the selection procedure should be uniform. This eliminates the appearance of bias or favoritism. Applicant notification is no different.

All candidates should be called since this speeds the process. It is better to schedule interviews in a block than to stretch them out over a week. This makes for better comparisons. But don't overload yourself. Three 60 minute interviews per day is more than enough.

When contacted for an interview, each candidate should be given the same information. Other than directions, nothing further should be added. Applicants' questions about what to expect should be politely refused. Giving one candidate an edge over another may come back to haunt you. To eliminate temptation, a receptionist or someone not affiliated with the process should do the calling.

Rejections

Every applicant who has been interviewed should receive a response. When candidates have been eliminated, they should be notified within two to three days. Notification should take the form of a letter such as the one below. You are not obligated to explain your reasons for rejection and volunteering such information is just asking for trouble.

Sample Rejection Letters

Dear.........,

Thank you for applying for the position of......... with Digi-Lectronics.

We were fortunate to receive a number of applications from highly qualified individuals. Our decision, which was difficult, has been made.

We will retain your application for six months in the event a similar position becomes available. Please accept our regrets and best wishes for success in your job search.

Sincerely,

....

Dear.........,

Thank you for your interest in Digi-Lectronics. We have reviewed your application. While we will continue hire for the opening of assembler, we have filled the current position with someone who more closely meets our requirements.

As additional assembler positions become available, we will once again review your application with others we have received. If at that time, we have an interest in interviewing you, we will be in touch.

Please accept our best wishes for continued success in your job search

Sincerely,

....

While you may not hire every candidate, each person rejected may eventually become a customer. It is always in our best interest to treat everyone with concern and courtesy. Applicants who feel dissatisfied with the hiring process, pass that feeling along to others. Don't let poorly handled rejections come back to haunt you at a later time.

III. Negotiating Offers and Compensation

Once the final decision has been made, the chosen candidate should be notified as soon as possible. When the offer has been made verbally, follow with a letter of confirmation stating the starting date and compensation agreed upon. Be careful not to include anything in the letter that would imply permanence. New hires may be full-time, but not forever.

Other sections of the letter may also create concerns. The courts for instance, have held that if a salary is stated as an annual amount, the employee may not be fired for a one year period. They have also held that if a letter of offer says that a new employees performance will be reviewed in six months, then the employee must be retained for at least that long. To avoid these situations, always give salary in monthly or weekly terms and indicate that performance will be reviewed periodically. Always end the letter with the statement, "This letter does not constitute a specific term of employment."

Offering Strategies

In some situations, you may have to negotiate with the chosen candidate because they are in demand. Certain technical specialties continue to command higher salaries because of their availability. Negotiations for executive level candidates are also more complex. Here are a few tips:

Know Your Parameters before Negotiating

Do your homework. Research salaries and compensation in your area. Prepare a list of what you are willing to offer and stick to the plan. Attempting to wing the negotiations may cost you money and the candidate.

Get them to commit before the selection is made. If the applicant has responded to a posting that identified salary range, you can assume they are accepting the salary range. If the candidate is exceptional, consider offering one or two percent over the advertised salary. This should lock them in since they applied for the position at a set salary range.

A second strategy is to ask candidates about their compensation demands during the interview process: "What do you think you're worth?" This will immediately give you an indication of their expectations.

Offer non-monetary perks. Make a list of factors which may attract good candidates such as working conditions, an office, a larger operating budget and more influence in decision-making.

Offer moving expenses and mortgage assistance. For those in middle management, this can be very helpful. Your company may be able to obtain better rates than an individual.

Build incentives and bonuses into compensation. You may tie performance to compensation. This saves you money and allows them the opportunity to increase their income.

A more expensive but very popular strategy is to offer a "signing bonus" where the candidate is offered a flat sum up front.

Offer a contract. Although very few companies offer contracts to new employees, this offer of security may be just the incentive to land an exceptional candidate. Contracts may also be offered after a period of time as an incentive.

Don't oversell the position. While you may think you have the perfect candidate, be careful not to offer so much that the offer is taken on money alone. If the candidate has some misgivings about the position, it is better to address these up front than to allow them to smolder.

A candidate who takes a position simply because of fantastic compensation may leave a short time later if initial difficulties are not resolved. Money is not the answer to every concern. High-demand candidates sometimes take positions where they can be challenged, in spite of less-than-sterling compensation.

Refusals

Unfortunately, your first choices may not always accept the offer. Once again, they are evaluating you as you are them. If you have not heard a reply within a day or two of making the offer, contact the candidate once again. Ask if there are any questions or concerns that might be resolved.

There is always the possibility that the candidate will hold out for additional compensation or conditions. Be careful not to over-commit yourself in this situation. In fields where there is a shortage of well-trained candidates, the individual may just be playing games to see how high you will go. Is this a person you really want on your team?

If more than one candidate is turning down your offer, it is best to re-evaluate the company's recruiting techniques. Are you asking for too much? Are you promising too much up front? Are you mis-representing the position? Before proceeding with another search, perform a reality check on how your process is working.

IV. The Decision-making Checklist

_____1. Have you developed a procedure in writing, for selecting managerial and non-managerial employees?

_____2. Have you developed candidate evaluation forms for the selection process?

_____3. Are you maintaining a file for every search containing the candidate evaluation forms on all rejected applicants?

_____4. Do you notify candidates in a timely fashion of both acceptance and rejection?

_____5. Have you had all correspondence pertaining to job offers and rejections reviewed by an attorney for inappropriate statements or commitments?

_____6. Are you _fully_ prepared when negotiating offers of employment?

A p p e n d i x **A**

Sample Interview Questions

How applicants answer a question can be just as important as what they say. Everything including eye contact, voice inflection, sincerity, enthusiasm and confidence play a role in helping to determine suitability. While most applicants can tell you what you want to hear, they can't hide natural non-verbal traits. Use your intuition. If the words sound okay, but something doesn't feel right, probe deeper. If it still doesn't feel right, there probably isn't a match, no matter what they say!

Take care to make these questions your own. Tailor them for your use. Experiment with new questions occasionally to see which will work better *in your setting*. The questions in this appendix are divided into two categories: Questions for non-supervisory positions and questions for supervisory positions. You are however, encouraged to review both sections before selecting the questions you wish to ask.

Nonsupervisiory

About the Job for Which They Are Applying

How did you find out about our company?
How did you find out about this job?
What do you know about this job?
What do you know about our company?
What do you know about our industry?

Why did you apply for this position?

How does this job fit into your career plans?

Why should I be worried about hiring you?

What would you expect your duties to be for a job as a _____?

What would expect to do on the first day on the job?

Tell me about your attendance record at your last job.

Is there anything that will prevent you from getting to work on time?

Tell me about your safety record on your last job.

If the employee working next to you had an accident, what would you do? (Why?)

If a fire suddenly broke out in the plant, what would you do?

What questions do you have about the job and/or working for us?

What do you know about the products we offer?

How would you like our company to assist you if you join us?

What would you say are the broad responsibilities of a _____?

"What would you say are the major qualities this job demands?" or "What would you say are the traits a good _____ would possess?

What are you looking for in your next job?

How long will it take you to make a contribution?

Explain your understanding of the job's responsibilities.

What kind of work interests you the most?

Tell me what you think a typical day would be like.

What do you think the position earns?

How will this job help you reach your long-term and career goals?

How do you define a successful career ?

Are you willing to relocate for the company?

What other functional, day-to-day activities were you involved with that we haven't discussed?

Applicant's Work Experience

Have you held other positions like the one you are applying for? Tell me about them.

If yes, what is the most important thing you learned that you can bring to this job?

Tell me about your last (or present) job. (Encourage them to discuss details. It will reveal work habits.)

What did you enjoy most about your last (or present) job?

What did you enjoy least about your last (or present) job?

What were the biggest pressures on your last job?

If there were two things you could change in your last (or present) job, what would they be and how would you change them?

Why did you leave your last job? (or Why do you wish to leave your present job?)

Why do you think you were successful in your last job?

How has your present (or last) job changed while you've held it?

Please describe your last (or present) boss' management style.

If you could make one constructive suggestion to management, what would it be?

What other people do you deal with in your present (or past) job?

If I asked your boss to evaluate your performance, what would s/he say?

What qualifications do you have that make you successful in this field?

What has been the most interesting job or project so far in your career?

What have you learned from previous jobs?

What is your boss's title and what are your boss's functions?

Please describe for me a typical day on your current job.

How do your previous work experiences prepare you for this position?

What aspects of your work do you consider most crucial?

Of all the work you have done, where have you been most successful?

Describe to me how your job relates to the overall goals of your department and company.

What are the most repetitive tasks in your job?

What special skills or knowledge did you need to perform these duties?

What decisions or judgment calls did you have to make in these areas?

What was the most important project you worked on at that job?

Did you work much alone in your previous job?

Applicant's Leadership/Management Potential

Tell me about a situation where you had to pull a team together successfully.

How effectively did your boss handle evaluations?

Do you set goals for yourself?

What have you done to reach it?

How do you organize yourself for day-to-day activities?

How many hours a week do you find it necessary to work to get your job done?

How do you plan your day?

Tell me about a system of working you have used and what it was like? What did/didn't you like about it?

Tell me about a method you've developed for accomplishing a job. What were its strengths and weaknesses?

What have you done to become more effective in your position?

In what areas could your boss have done a better job?

Describe the best manager you ever had.

Describe the worst manager you ever had.

Have you ever been placed in charge of the department, store, etc.?

What did you like about being in charge?

What did you not like about being in charge?

If you were placed in charge again what would you do differently?

How did your peers act toward you when you were in charge?

Communication Skills

When you are assigned to work with new people, how do you go about getting to know them and how they work?

How do you get along with your present boss?

What type of person is the hardest for you to get along with?

Tell me about your experience in working on teams.

What can you contribute to a team?

What do you get out of working on a team?

Do you prefer working alone or with others?

What kind of people annoy you most? (Note: The applicant is probably the opposite of the type of person given as a response.)

How did you get along with your former boss?

What sort of person would you least like to work with? (Note: Again, the candidate is probably the opposite of the kind of person given as a response.)

Tell me about a work situation that required excellent communication skills.

What sort of person do you enjoy working for?

How well/often do you communicate with the person who receives the output of your work?

Define cooperation.

How important was communication and interaction with others on this job?

What other titles and departments did you have dealings with. What were the difficulties you encountered there?

What was more important on your job, written or oral communication?

How many levels of management did you interact with? What was your communication about?

Do you prefer to speak with someone or send a memo?

When do you have trouble communicating with people?

Conflict/Persuasion Skills

Have you ever been in a dispute with a supervisor? What was it about and how was it resolved?

Have you ever been in a dispute with a co-worker? What was it about and how was it resolved?

Describe the best person who ever worked with you.

How do you handle conflicts?

What are the disadvantages of your chosen field?

Have you ever worked with a group like this before? What was it like? or How did you handle it?

Tell me about a time when you needed to get an understanding of another's situation before you could get your job done. How did you get the understanding, and what problems did you encounter?

Are you able to predict a person's behavior based on your reading of them?

Tell me about a specific accomplishment you have achieved as a group member.

What difficulties do you have in tolerating people with different backgrounds and interests from yours?

When you joined your last company and met the group for the first time, how did you feel? How did you get on with them?

How would you define a conducive work atmosphere?

As a member of a department, how do you see your role as team builder?

Tell me about a time when you came up with a new method or idea. How did you get it approved and implemented?

Can you think of a time when another idea or project was rejected. Why was it rejected and what did you do about it?

I would be interested to hear about an occasion when your work or an idea was criticized?

Tell me about a situation when people were making emotional decisions about your project? What happened and how did you handle it?

Tell me about an occasion when there were objections to your ideas. What did you do to convince management of your point of view?

Have you ever been in a situation where people overrule you or won't let you get a word in edgeways? How did you respond?

Tell me about an occasion when you felt it necessary to convince your department to change a procedure.

What are some of the things about which you and your boss disagreed?

What are some of the things your boss did that you disliked?

Education & Training

What was your overall grade point average in school?

Do you feel your grades are an accurate reflection of your work? If not, why not?

What subject did you do the best in? Why?

What subject did you have the most trouble with? Why?

What subject did you like the best? Why?

What subject did you dislike the most? Why?

What skills did you learn in school that will help you on this job?

Were you involved in extracurricular activities? If yes, which ones?

What have you learned from your extracurricular activities?

If you could do so, how would you plan your academic studies differently?

What prompted you to choose _____ as your major?

What courses do you think are directly transferable to the job?

What kind of skills were acquired as a result of your training?

What extracurricular positions have you held?

What have you learned through volunteer leadership?

Do you think that your extracurricular activities were worth the time you devoted to them? Why?

Can you forget your education and start from scratch?

What plans do you have for additional training or education?

Personal Traits

What kind of person do you get along with best?

What ways do you find to tolerate people who have different backgrounds and values from yours?

What makes a job enjoyable for you?

What do you want out of a job?

What qualities would you bring to this job that others would not?

Where do you feel you need to improve?

If you worked for the perfect boss, what would this person be like?

What do you consider important in a job?

How do you define doing a good job?

What is your greatest strength? Worst deficiency?

What books or magazines do you read?

What do you think are the most serious problems facing business today?

What are you best known for?

From whom have you learned the most?

Tell me about a time when you conformed to a policy with which you disagreed.

Which American business person do you most admire and why?

Have you ever taken a public-speaking course?

What do you do to keep in good physical condition?

Tell me about a responsibility you have enjoyed.

Describe a project that required a high amount of energy over an extended period of time.

What did you do to keep your enthusiasm up?

Tell me about an occasion when your performance didn't live up to your expectations?

How long will you stay with the company?

What books have had the greatest effect on your business life?

How do you define a successful career?

Is this the type of career you want for yourself?

How do you take direction?

For what have you been most frequently criticized?

Recall for me a time when those around you were not being as honest or direct as they should have been. What did you do?

When was the last time you got really angry? Tell me about the last time you felt anger on the job?

In what ways did your manager contribute to your decision to leave your current job?

Problem Solving/Decision Making Skills

Tell me about a specific situation where you prevented a problem before it occurred.

What is the most difficult task you have had to complete? (Ask them to explain in detail.)

What do you do when you're having trouble solving a problem?

What is the biggest decision you have had to make in the past year?

What kinds of things do you find difficult to do?

What kinds of decisions do you find particularly hard to make?

Describe some of the emergencies that forced you to rearrange your time in some of your previous jobs.

What problem-solution situation are you most proud of?

Describe a situation that required you to use fact-finding skills.

What was the last truly innovative suggestion you made for your firm?

What has been your most important work-related idea?

What kind of things bother you most about your job?

Tell me about a problem you experienced in this area, something you found difficult to handle.

What was the most complex report you ever had to write?

Who caused you the most problems in executing your tasks? With whom were you most comfortable?

Tell me about a time when a team fell apart. Why did it happen? What did you do?

Have you ever had to build motivation or team spirit with co-workers?

Tell me about a complex problem you had to deal with.

Where/to whom do you turn for help? How do you overcome the problem?

Tell me about a job or project where you had to gather information from many different sources and then create something with the information.

How do you organize and plan for major projects? Recall for me a major project you worked on. How did you organize and plan for it?

Tell me about a time when you failed to reach a goal?

How many projects can you handle at a time?

Describe a typical day for me. What problems do you normally experience in getting things done?

Think of a crisis situation where things got out of control. Why did it happen and what was your role in the chain of events?

What do you do when you have a great deal of work to accomplish in a short time-span? How have you reacted?

What do you do when there is a decision to be made and no procedure exists.

Give me an example of a time when management had to change a plan or approach you were committed to.

Tell me about a time when, rather than following instructions, you went about a task in your own way. What happened?

Your boss is going on vacation for a month, and although it isn't in your job description to do so, she asks you to work for another manager in her absence. What would you say and do? Are you prepared to fill in for someone who has different, even lower-level, responsibilities?

Your boss dictates several letters, tells you to sign them, and, as he rushes out the door for a trip, asks you to include a form. You realize after he has left that you don't know what form he meant. What do you do?

Money Questions

How much money are you making?

What I am really looking for is your salary, not the value of your benefit package or other fringes.

How much money do you want?

In your professional opinion, how much do you think a job like this should pay?

If you went to your boss for a raise, why would you be doing it?

Tell me about your salary history.

Personal Motivation

What has been your greatest accomplishment in a work environment and why?

How do you feel about your present workload?

Give me an example of a situation where you had to go above and beyond the call of duty to get something done.

What do you do when things are slow at work?

A year from now, what might your boss say about your work for our company during a performance review?

What have you learned from your mistakes?

What motivates you to put forth your greatest effort?

What two or three accomplishments have given you the most satisfaction? Why?

How can we best reward you for doing a good job?

Why do you think you'll be successful in this job?

What gives you pride?

Tell me about a time when you went "out on a limb" in a job.

What concerns should I have about hiring you?

What do you think it takes to be successful in this company?

Why should we hire you?

Why are you giving up your current job?

Why did you choose your particular field?

What is more important to you: the salary or the job itself?

What are the disadvantages associated with your chosen field?

What do you think determines a person's progress in a firm?

Do you think you would be underemployed if you accepted this position?

What are your goals—both short-term and long-term?

What are your hobbies or pastimes?

Describe your "dream" job?

What motivates you?

How intuitive are you?

How do you cope with the inevitable stresses and pressures of the job?

If you were me, would you hire you? Why?

Have you ever thought about starting your own company?

What ways have you discovered to improve your productivity?

What did you find most frustrating on your last job?

What are your short-and long-term objectives or goals?

What kinds of things would you want to avoid in future jobs?

What kinds of developmental experiences might be necessary to reach your goals?

What do you think has accounted for the success you've had so far in your career?

What would you say are some of the basic factors that motivate you in your work?

How have you grown in your job over the last few years?

How did you handle your biggest career disappointment?

What job in our company would you choose if you were free to do so?

What job in our company do you want to work toward?

What else should I know about your qualifications for this job? or What else should I know about you? or Is there anything else you want to tell me?

How did you feel about your workload at that company? How did you divide your time among your major areas of responsibility?

Have you discussed your desire to leave with your boss?

In what ways did your boss contribute to your desire to leave?

Why were you fired?

Why have you changed jobs so frequently?

Some people feel that spending so much time on one job demonstrates a lack of initiative. How do you feel about that?

What have you learned from jobs you have held?

What reservations do you have about working here? What would your references say?

What personal qualities do you think are necessary to make a success of this job?

Give me an example from your current job that demonstrates your persistence.

How do you feel about your progress to date?

In hindsight, in what ways could you have improved your progress?

How do you rank among your peers?

What have you done that you are proud of?

Tell me about a project that really got you excited?

What are some of the things you find difficult to do?

When you've a great deal of work to do that requires extra effort and time, where does your energy come from?

Is it ever necessary to go above and beyond the call of duty to get your job done?

How was your approach different from that of others in the same job?

When you have been in difficult and crisis situations, which areas of your professional skills do you vow to work on further?

Can you recall a time when you went back to a failed project to give it another shot? Why did you do it and what happened?

Why aren't you earning more at your age?

What can you do for us that someone else cannot do?

Are you willing to go where the company sends you?

What are your reservations about living/working here?

How would working evenings affect you?

How would travel affect you?

How did your boss get the best out of you?

Would you like to have your boss' job?

How do your work habits change when your boss is absent?

What problems do you experience when working alone?

How do the work habits of others change when the boss is absent?

Tell me about a time when there was a decision to be made and your boss was absent.

Tell me about a time you felt adequately recognized for your contributions.

What kind of rewards are most satisfying to you?

How does this affect what you do on the job? How does this affect the effort you put into your job?

What can you do for us that someone else cannot do?

Are you looking for a temporary or a permanent job?

What have you done that show initiative and willingness to work?

How did you spend your vacations while at school?

What ways do you find work interferes with your personal life?

Have you ever found it necessary to sacrifice personal plans in favor of your professional responsibilities?

Supervisory/Management

About the Job

How did you find out about our company?

How did you find out about this job?

What do you know about this job?

What do you know about our company?

What do you know about the products we offer?

What do you know about our industry?

Why did you apply for this position?

How does this job fit into your career plans?

Why should I be worried about hiring you?

What would you expect your duties to be for a job as a _____?

What would expect to do on the first day on the job?

What questions do you have about the job and/or working for us?

How would you like our company to assist you if you join us?

What would you say are the broad responsibilities of _____?

What would you say are the major qualities this job demands?

What would you say are the traits a good _____ would possess?

What are you looking for in your next job?

How long will it take you to make a contribution?

Why do you think you might want to live in the community where our company is located?

Are you willing to spend at least six months as a trainee?

Work Experience

Have you held other positions like the one you are applying for? Tell me about them.

If yes, what is the most important thing you learned that you can bring to this job?

Tell me about your last (or present) job. (Encourage them to discuss details. It will reveal work habits.)

What did you enjoy most about your last (or present) job?

What did you enjoy least about your last (or present) job?

What were the biggest pressures on your last job?

If there were two things you could change in your last (or present) job, what would they be and how would you change them?

Why did you leave your last job? (or Why do you wish to leave your present job?)

Why do you think you were successful in your last job?

How has your present (or last) job changed while you've held it?

Please describe your last (or present) boss' management style.

If you could make one constructive suggestion to management, what would it be?

What other people do you deal with in your present (or past) job?

If I asked your boss to evaluate your performance, what would s/he say?

In all the jobs you've held, where do you think you have been the most successful?

Tell me about a situation where an crisis occurred and you have to shift priorities and workload quickly.

How do you feel about your present workload?

What are the most repetitive tasks you do on your present job?

If there were two things you could change in your job, what would they be and how would you change them?

Why do you think you were successful in your last job?

How has your present (or last) job changed while you've held it?

In what ways has your manager contributed to your choosing to leave your present job?

How do you feel your present boss can do a better job?

How will your supervisor react when to resign from your present job?

What qualifications do you have that make you successful in this field?

What has been the most interesting job or project so far in your career?

Describe the most significant report or presentation you have had to prepare.

What have you learned from previous jobs?

What is your boss's title and what are your boss's functions?

Please describe for me a typical day on your current job.

How do your previous work experiences prepare you for this position?

What aspects of your work do you consider most crucial?

Of all the work you have done, where have you been most successful?

Describe to me how your job relates to the overall goals of your department and company.

What are the most repetitive tasks in your job?

What special skills or knowledge did you need to perform these duties?

What decisions or judgment calls did you have to make in these areas?

What was the most important project you worked on at that job?

Did you work much alone in your previous job?

What responsibilities do you hold in relation to other departments?

Communication Skills

When you are assigned to work with new people, how do you go about getting to know them and how they work?

How do you get along with your present boss?

What type of person is the hardest for you to get along with?

Tell me about your experience in working on teams.

What can you contribute to a team?

What do you get out of working on a team?

Do you prefer working alone or with others?

What kind of people annoy you most? (Note: The applicant is probably the opposite of the type of person given as a response.)

How did you get along with your former boss?

What sort of person would you least like to work with? (Note: Again, the candidate is probably the opposite of the kind of person given as a response.)

Tell me about a work situation that required excellent communication skills.

What sort of person do you enjoy working for?

How well/often do you communicate with the person who receives the output of your work?

Define cooperation.

How important was communication and interaction with others on this job?

What other titles and departments did you have dealings with. What were the difficulties you encountered there?

What was more important on your job, written or oral communication?

How many levels of management did you interact with? What was your communication about?

Do you prefer to speak with someone or send a memo?

When do you have trouble communicating with other people?

Conflict/Persuasion Skills

Have you ever been in a dispute with a supervisor? What was it about and how was it resolved?

Have you ever been in a dispute with a co-worker? What was it about and how was it resolved?

Have you ever been in a dispute with someone you supervised? What was it about and how was it resolved?

Describe the best person who ever worked for you or with you.

How do you handle conflicts?

Have you ever worked with a group like this before? What was it like? or How did you handle it?

Tell me about a time when you needed to get an understanding of another's situation before you could get your job done. How did you get the understanding, and what problems did you encounter?

Are you able to predict a person's behavior based on your reading of them?

Tell me about a specific accomplishment you have achieved as a group member.

What difficulties do you have in tolerating people with different backgrounds and interests from yours?

When you joined your last company and met the group for the first time, how did you feel? How did you get on with them?

Define cooperation.

How would you define a conducive work atmosphere?

As a member of a department, how do you see your role as team builder?

Tell me about a time when you came up with a new method or idea. How did you get it approved and implemented?

Can you think of a time when another idea or project was rejected. Why was it rejected and what did you do about it?

I would be interested to hear about an occasion when your work or an idea was criticized?

Tell me about a situation when people were making emotional decisions about your project? What happened and how did you handle it?

Tell me about an occasion when there were objections to your ideas. What did you do to convince management of your point of view?

Have you ever been in a situation where people overrule you or won't let you get a word in edgeways?

Tell me about an occasion when you felt it necessary to convince your department to change a procedure.

Education & Training

What was your overall grade point average in school?

Do you feel your grades are an accurate reflection of your work? If not, why not?

What subject did you do the best in? Why?

What subject did you have the most trouble with? Why?

What subject did you like the best? Why?

What subject did you dislike the most? Why?

What skills did you learn in school that will help you on this job?

Were you involved in extracurricular activities? If yes, which ones?

What have you learned from your extracurricular activities?

If you could do so, how would you plan your academic studies differently?

What books have had the greatest effect on your business development? Why?

What prompted you to choose _____ as your major?

What courses do you think are directly transferable to the job?

What kind of skills were acquired as a result of that training?

What extracurricular offices have you held?

Do you think that your extracurricular activities were worth the time you devoted to them? Why?

Can you forget your education and start from scratch?

What additional education or training do you plan to pursue?

Personal Traits

What kind of person do you get along with best?

What ways do you find to tolerate people who have different backgrounds and values from yours?

What makes a job enjoyable for you?

What do you want out of a job?

What qualities would you bring to this job that others would not?

Where do you feel you need to improve?

If you worked for the perfect boss, what would this person be like?

What do you consider important in a job?

How do you define doing a good job?

In what kind of work environment are you most comfortable?

Under what conditions do you work best?

How have the jobs you have held in the past prepared you for larger responsibilities in a new position?

What goals, other than those related to your occupation have you set for yourself over the next ten years?

What is your greatest strength? Worst deficiency?

Are you willing to relocate for the company?

What books or magazines do you read?

What do you think are the most serious problems facing business today?

What are you best known for?

From whom have you learned the most?

Tell me about a time when you conformed to a policy with which you disagreed.

What American business person do you most admire and why?

Have you ever taken a public-speaking course?

What do you do to keep in good physical condition?

What are the disadvantages of your chosen field?

What other functional, day-to-day activities were you involved with that we haven't discussed?

Tell me about a responsibility you have enjoyed.

Describe a project that required a high amount of energy over an extended period of time.

What did you do to keep your enthusiasm up?

Tell me about an occasion when your performance didn't live up to your expectations?

How long will you stay with the company?

What books have had the greatest effect on your business life?

How do you define a successful career?

Is this the type of career you want for yourself?

How do you take direction?

What are some of the things about which you and your boss disagreed?

What are some of the things your boss did that you disliked?

For what have you been most frequently criticized?

Recall for me a time when those around you were not being as honest or direct as they should have been. What did you do?

When was the last time you got really angry?

Tell me about the last time you felt anger on the job?

In what ways did your manager contribute to your decision to leave this job?

Problem Solving/Decision Making Skills

Tell me about a specific situation where you prevented a problem before it occurred.

What is the most difficult task you have had to complete? (Ask them to explain in detail.)

What do you do when you're having trouble solving a problem?

What is the biggest decision you have had to make in the past year?

What kinds of things do you find difficult to do?

What kinds of decisions do you find particularly hard to make?

Tell me about a situation where you had to deal with a particularly difficult grievance.

How do you make important decisions?

Tell me about a situation where you overcame objections of other people and convinced them your plan was best.

Tell me about how you have handled a major problem.

Tell me about a time when you had to make a quick decision and how you went about making it.

Describe some of the emergencies that forced you to rearrange your time in some of your previous jobs.

What problem-solution situation are you most proud of?

Describe a situation that required you to use fact-finding skills.

What was the last truly innovative suggestion you made for your firm?

What has been your most important work-related idea?

What kind of things bother you most about your job?

Tell me about a problem you experienced in this area, something you found difficult to handle.

What was the most complex report you ever had to write?

Who caused you the most problems in executing your tasks? With whom were you most comfortable?

Tell me about a time when a team fell apart. Why did it happen? What did you do?

Have you ever had to build motivation or team spirit with co-workers?

Tell me about a complex problem you had to deal with.

Where/to whom do you turn for help? How do you overcome the problem?

Tell me about a job or project where you had to gather information from many different sources and then create something with the information.

How do you organize and plan for major projects? Recall for me a major project you worked on. How did you organize and plan for it?

Tell me about a time when you failed to reach a goal.

How many projects can you handle at a time?

Describe a typical day for me. What problems do you normally experience in getting things done?

Think of a crisis situation where things got out of control. Why did it happen and what was your role in the chain of events?

What do you do when you have a great deal of work to accomplish in a short time-span? How have you reacted?

What do you do when there is a decision to be made and no procedure exists.

Give me an example of a time when management had to change a plan or approach you were committed to. How did you feel and how did you explain the change to your people

Money Questions

What salary do you expect to make in this position? What do you base that figure on?

How can we best reward you?

What is your current salary?

What do you expect to earning in five years?

How much money are you making?

What I am really looking for is your salary, not the value of your benefit package or other fringes.

How much money do you want?

In your professional opinion, how much do you think a job like this should pay?

If you went to your boss for a raise, why would you be doing it?

How would you justify a raise to your boss?

Besides salary, what other benefits are you looking for?

Do you have an interest in owning equity?

Have you ever worked on commission? Tell me about it.

Personal Motivation

What has been your greatest accomplishment in a work environment and why?

How do you feel about your present workload?

Give me an example of a situation where you had to go above and beyond the call of duty to get something done.

What do you do when things are slow at work?

A year from now, what might your boss say about your work for our company during a performance review?

What have you learned from your mistakes?

What motivates you to put forth your greatest effort?

What two or three accomplishments have given you the most satisfaction? Why?

How can we best reward you for doing a good job?

Why do you think you'll be successful in this job?

What gives you pride?

Tell me about a time when you went "out on a limb" in a job.

What concerns should I have about hiring you?

What do you think it takes to be successful in this company?

What criteria are you using to evaluate the company for which you would like to work?

How do you like to be managed?

How has your boss been able to get the best out of you?

Do you consider yourself successful? Why?

What have you done to become more effective in your present position?

How do you plan to achieve your career goals?

What are the most important rewards you expect from your career?

What kinds of rewards are most satisfying to you?

How do you determine success?

Why are you giving up your current job?

Why did you choose your particular field?

What is more important to you: the salary or the job itself?

What are the disadvantages associated with your chosen field?

What do you think determines a person's progress in a firm?

Do you think you would be underemployed if you accepted this position?

What are your goals—both short-term and long-term?

What are your hobbies or pastimes?

Describe your "dream" job?

What motivates you?

How intuitive are you?

How do you cope with the inevitable stresses and pressures of the job?

If you were me, would you hire you? Why?

Have you ever thought about starting your own company?

What ways have you discovered to improve your productivity?

What did you find most frustrating on your last job?

What are your short-and long-term objectives or goals?

What kinds of things would you want to avoid in future jobs?

What kinds of developmental experiences might be necessary to reach your goals?

What do you think has accounted for the success you've had so far in your career?

What would you say are some of the basic factors that motivate you in your work?

How have you grown in your job over the last few years?

How did you handle your biggest career disappointment?

What job in our company would you choose if you were free to do so?

What job in our company do you want to work toward?

How necessary is it for you to be creative on your job?

What else should I know about your qualifications for this job?

What else should I know about you?

Is there anything else you want to tell me?

How did you feel about your workload at that company? How did you divide your time among your major areas of responsibility?

Have you discussed your desire to leave with your boss?

In what ways did your boss contribute to your desire to leave?

Why were you fired?

Why have you changed jobs so frequently?

Some people feel that spending so much time on one job demonstrates a lack of initiative. How do you feel about that?

What have you learned from jobs you have held?

What reservations do you have about working here? What would your references say?

What personal qualities do you think are necessary to make a success of this job?

Give me an example from your current job that demonstrates your persistence.

How do you feel about your progress to date?

In hindsight, in what ways could you have improved your progress?

How do you rank among your peers?

What have you done that you are proud of?

Tell me about a project that really got you excited?

What are some of the things you find difficult to do?

When you've a great deal of work to do that requires extra effort and time, where does your energy come from?

Is it ever necessary to go above and beyond the call of duty to get your job done?

How was your approach different from that of others in the same job?

When you have been in difficult and crisis situations, which areas of your professional skills do you vow to work on further?

Can you recall a time when you went back to a failed project to give it another shot? Why did you do it and what happened?

Why aren't you earning more at your age?

What can you do for us that someone else cannot do?

Are you willing to go where the company sends you?

What are your reservations about living/working here?

How would working evenings affect you?

How would travel affect you?

How did your boss get the best out of you?

Would you like to have your boss' job?

How do your work habits change when your boss is absent?

What problems do you experience when working alone?

How do the work habits of others change when the boss is absent?

Tell me about a time when there was a decision to be made and your boss was absent.

Tell me about a time you felt adequately recognized for your contributions.

What kind of rewards are most satisfying to you?

How does this affect what you do on the job? How does this affect the effort you put into your job?

What can you do for us that someone else cannot do?

What have you done that show initiative and willingness to work?

How did you spend your vacations while at school?

Budgetary/Fiscal Management Skills

Do you perform employee salary reviews? If yes, what is your approach?

Are you in charge of the budget for your department?

If yes, tell me about how you budget for the year?

What problems do you have staying within your budget?

Are you involved in the overall budget planning for your organization?

What was your involvement in short-/mid-/long-term planning?

How do you quantify the results of your activities as manager?

Are you competent with electronic spreadsheet programs?

How do you deal with unanticipated expenses?

How do you defend the budget in your present position?

Tell me about a time when you had to ask for additional monies.

Tell me about a time when you had to restructure your budget in the middle of the year. What approach did you take?

How would you create a budget in the position for which you are applying?

Supervisory/Management Skills

Tell me about a situation where you had to pull a team together successfully.

How do you define the job of a manager?

Who reports to you and what functions do they perform?

What has been the employee turnover in your department over the past two years?

To what do you attribute this turnover?

What do you actively do to retain employees?

What programs have you put in place to build morale among those reporting to you?

What are the typical problems and grievances your staff bring you?

How do you go about assigning and scheduling projects and assignments?

What other organizational responsibilities do you have besides managing your department?

Describe your management style for me.

How do you measure your success as a manager?

What patterns have you observed in the turnover in your department?

How many people have you hired in the past two years? Into what positions?

What training have your performed on other people? How do you measure its success?

How do you determine which individuals need what training?

How do you plan your daily activities?

If you are hired for this job, how will you approach the first 30 days?

How do you keep your present staff informed of new developments and organizational decisions?

Describe the relationship that you feel should exist between a supervisor and those reporting to him/her.

What aspects of this job would you consider most crucial?

How have you allocated your time between the duties in your present job?

Tell me about the best manager you have ever had.

Tell me about the worst manager you have ever had.

Describe an innovative change you implemented in your last job.

Give me an example of a problem in which you and your boss disagreed over how to accomplish a goal.

Tell me about a project where you had to interact with people on different levels and how you coordinated that successfully.

Have you ever had to make unpopular management decisions? Tell me about one of these situations and how you handled it.

How long will it take for you to make a contribution in this position?

How do you cope when a decision has to be made and no procedure exists?

How, specifically, do you contribute toward an atmosphere of teamwork?

How would you define leadership?

What is your philosophy of business?

What can a department do to build teamwork?

What was the most creative work project you ever completed?

Do you manage your time well? Explain?

What are your views on quality?

Describe a time when you were able to have a positive influence on others.

How flexible are you?

What can be done about employees entering the work force without proper skills?

Do you train others well? Please give me an example of your effectiveness.

How well do you think on your feet?

How effectively did your boss handle evaluations?

What level of management are you most comfortable with? What levels are you most uncomfortable with?

Do you set goals for yourself?

What have you done to reach it?

How do you organize yourself for day-to-day activities?

How many hours a week do you find it necessary to work to get your job done?

How do you plan your day?

Tell me about a system of working you have used and what it was like? What did/didn't you like about it?

Tell me about a method you've developed for accomplishing a job. What were its strengths and weaknesses?

What have you done to become more effective in your position?

Tell me about a directive that really challenged you.

In what areas could your boss have done a better job?

If you could have made one constructive suggestion to management, what would it have been?

How would you define the job of a manager?

Who performed salary reviews on these people?

What type of turnover was most frequent, terminations or resignations?

When were resignations most likely to occur?

Have you ever trained other people?

How do you analyze the training needs of your department or of specific individuals?

How do you keep your staff aware of information and company activities that might affect them?

Have you ever had an employee suddenly start acting out of character?

Tell me about a program you introduced to improve morale.

How do you motivate staff?

Tell me about how you motivated your staff when faced with a specific tight deadline.

What methods have you found successful in setting job objectives for subordinates?

Have you ever had to make unpopular decisions?

Tell me about a time when an emergency/directive from above caused you to reschedule workload/projects. How did you feel?

What method did you use in performing salary reviews?

How did you schedule projects, assignments, and vacations.

How would you characterize your management style?

Tell me about a time when people were making emotional decisions about your projects. What happened and what did you do?

Hiring Skills

What do you do to orient new employees into your department?

If you were hiring someone for this job, what qualities would you look for?

How many people have you hired?

How do you plan to interview?

Tell me what questions you would ask, or techniques you would use, to establish if the person was willing to do the job?

What steps do you normally take to get a new employee oriented to the new ways of doing things?

How would you seek applicants for open positions within your department?

Tell me about how you would budget for recruiting.

What do you look for on a resume or application?

Tell me about your biggest hiring success.

Tell me about your biggest hiring mistake.

How do you go about checking references?

On what criteria do you base hiring decisions?

How could we improve the hiring process we are using to select a person for this position?

Discipline/Termination Skills

Do you have the authority to terminate people? If yes, describe your approach.

How do you maintain discipline within your department?

How many employees have you fired in the past year?

Tell me about the last time you fired someone? What were the reasons?

How many people have you fired?

What is the most common cause of termination?

How do you maintain discipline in your department? What special problems do you have with the day-to-day management of your staff?

What are the typical problems and grievances that your staff bring to you? How do you handle them?

In working with others, how do you go about getting an understanding of them?

Sales

Telephone Skills

How does it differ from outside sales?

What strategies do you use to get through the secretary or receptionist?

Have you ever sold anything over the telephone?

What special skills or techniques are necessary to be successful over the telephone?

Tell me about a time when you called a complete stranger on the phone. How did you initiate a discussion?

When getting through to a sales prospect for the first time on the phone, what roadblocks can you expect the clerical staff to put in your way and how do you handle them?

How much time do you spend on the telephone in your job?

What services or products have you sold over the phone?

How many phone calls do you make in a day?

Demonstrate your telephone sales technique for me.

Where do you find your telephone leads?

What do you enjoy about telephone sales?

What do you despise about telephone sales?

Tell me about the person who supervised your telephone sales.

What can you do to improve your telephone sales technique?

Prospecting Skills

What are people's reasons for buying a particular product or service?

How do you plan effective use of your day?

Tell me about why you plan your day in that way.

How do you overcome the difficult periods that face everyone in sales?

How long does it take you from initial contact to close a sale?

What is your ratio of initial contacts to actual sales presentations?

What kind of people do you like to sell to? Why?

What kind of people do you not like to sell to? Why?

How do you manage to sell to those people?

How would you go about identifying customers in a new market?

How do you initiate discussion with a complete stranger?

What percentage of your sales calls result in full presentations?

How long does it typically take you from initial contact to close the sale?

Closing Skills

How would you approach the sales of our products?

Why can you sell for us in a way that no one else can?

Tell me about a time when you almost lost a sale and then fought hard to get it back.

What are the five most common objections you face and how do you deal with them?

What percentage of your sales calls result in sales?

Tell me about your most difficult sale and how you approached it.

What was the most surprising objection you ever received, and how did you handle it?

What are the very toughest objections you have to meet in your job?

Sell me this pen.

Tell me about a time when all seemed lost in an important sale. What did you do to weather the crisis?

Give me an example of a sale that was, for all intents and purposes, lost. How did you turn the situation around and make the sale?

Customer Service Skills

What is your philosophy of customer service.

Tell me about your worst customer service dilemma and how you over came it.

How do you turn an occasional buyer into a regular buyer? Have you ever taken over an existing territory/desk? What was the volume when you started? What was it when you left?

How involved should a company be with its customers?

I'd be interested to hear about a difficult collection problem you have experienced.

What do you stress to support staff about customer service?

How do you deal with customers who think they are right even when they are wrong?

What is the customer service attitude in you present organization?

Where did you learn your customer sales skills and philosophy?

Tell me about a difficult collection problem you've had and how you dealt with it.

What kind of people do you like to sell to?

What type of people don't you like to sell to? How do you manage to sell to these people?

How do you cope with customers who ask for unreasonable discounts or service?

How have you handled customers who took advantage of sales support staff?

How do you encourage customers to pay on time?

Sales Management Skills

By what percentage have you increased the volume in your territory since you took it over?

Describe a typical day.

How do you plan your day?

Why is it important to prioritize/

Give me an example of when it was necessary to reach a goal in a short period of time and how you planned to achieve it.

For what have you been most frequently criticized, and by whom?

How large a client base do you need to maintain to keep sales on an even keel?

Have you ever broken in a new territory/desk for your company? How did you like it? How did you approach the job?

How would you go about identifying customers in a new market?

How do you prefer to go about securing new prospects and clients?

What steps are involved in selling your product?

How much time do you spend doing paperwork and other non-selling activities?

What is the one thing you could do right now to improve your sales management skills?

Marketing Skills

Why do people buy a product or service?

What do you know about our product line?

Tell me about how you reach your present customer base.

Tell me about how you would reach our customers.

Do you have a marketing budget in your present position? Tell me what it is composed of.

Here is one of our products. How would you go about marketing it?

What media contacts do you have that would help us market our products?

Tell me about your biggest marketing success.

Tell me about your biggest marketing flop. What happened?

Motivation for Sales

What do you dislike about most sales?

Why have you chosen to become a salesperson?

What rewards do you find most satisfying?

What have been your highest and lowest rankings in your current sales force?

Tell me about a time when you exceeded all expectations and why you think it happened.

Compare yourself to your peers.

How do you feel when you don't meet your quota?

What awards have you won as a sales person?

How do you feel about out of town/overnight travel?

What do you dislike about most sales?

What kind of rewards are most satisfying to you?

How do you keep yourself going when everyone else is having a bad day/is unorganized/is depressed?

Have you ever worked in an environment where people took advantage when the boss was away? How did you handle it?

How smart are you compared to your peers?

How articulate are you?

How well-dressed are you?

How witty are you?

How do you rank professionally?

How tenacious are you?

How well do you accept disappointment?

I'd be interested to hear of a time when you proved yourself to be more tenacious than your peers.

What have been your highest and lowest rankings in your current/last sales force?

Share with me an example of surpassing what was expected of you from your employer.

I'd be interested to hear about a specific time when you greatly exceeded the norm.

What different types of customer have you called on, and what titles have you sold to in these companies?

Tell me about your most crushing failure.

Give me a specific example of a time you were rejected and how you handled it.

All of us have failed to meet a quota at one point or another. When you don't meet your goals, how do you handle it?

Tell me about a time when you exhibited persistence but still couldn't reach a carefully planned goal.

What will you do if I don't hire you?

Federal Recordkeeping Requirements

Statute	Employers Affected	Requirements	Period of Retention	When Required	Posting Required
Title VII Civil Rights Act 1964 **Americans with Disabilities Act of 1990**	Employers with 15 or more employees Employers of 25 or more employees-July 26, 1992. Employers of 15-24 or more employees-July 26, 1994	Retain all personnel and employee records Retain records relevant to a charge of discrimination. Maintain records of impact of employment decisions, including hiring, termination, promotion.	Minimum of 6 months or after the last record was made, whichever is longer. Until final disposition of the charge.	Annually by March 31st. Do on an annual basis.	Official EEO poster available from any EEO district office. This consolidated poster will also cover ADEA, Executive Order 11246, Rehabilitation Act of 1974 and the ADA. It also covers a portion of FLSA. (See FLSA.)
	Employers with 100 or more employees (except state & local governments, primary and secondary school systems, institutions of higher education, Indian tribes, tax exempt private membership clubs other than labor organizations, and employees is Puerto Rico, Guam and the Virgin Islands.)	File Employer Information Report EEO-1.			
Title VII Civil Rites Act 1964 (continued)	Employers with 100 or more employees, and government agencies, labor organizations, and apprenticeship committees involved in employee selection. Joint labor-management apprenticeship committees with: 1. five or more apprentices enrolled and 2. at least one sponsoring employer who employs 25 or more members. 3. at least one sponsoring union with 25 or more members. Banking and financial institutions that serve as depositories of government funds in any amount or as issuing or paying agents for U.S. Savings Bonds. (Except those in Puerto Rico, Guam or the Virgin Islands.)	Maintain records of impact of employment decisions and calculator impact under the "4/5 rule" on a job-by-job basis. File Apprenticeship Information Report EEO-2. File employer information report EEO-1.		Impact should be measured at least annually. Annually by Sept. 30. Annually by March 31st.	
	Federal contractors and subcontractors with 50 or more employees and at least $50,000 in contracts. (Except those in Puerto Rico, Guam or the Virgin Islands.)	File Employer information report EEO-1.		Within 30 days after contract is awarded and annually by March 31st thereafter.	

Statute	Employers Affected	Requirements	Period of Retention	When Required	Posting Required
Executive Order 11246	Federal government contractors and subcontractors: contractors under federally assisted construction contracts.	Written affirmative action programs and supporting documentation. Other records pertaining to EEO compliance including validation and use of testing. Compliance with construction industry EEO plans and requirements. No particular forms of retention specified.			
Age Discrimination in Employment Act	Employers with more than 20 employees and engaged in interstate commerce.	Retain all payroll records. Personnel records relation to applications, resumes and other responses to job advertising for full-time, part-time and temporary positions including records pertaining to failure or refusal to hire. Promotion, demotion, transfer, selection for training, layoff, recall, or discharge records. Record of job orders submitted to employment agencies unions. Test papers in connection with employer administered aptitude or other employment test. Physical examination results in connection with a personnel action. Job advertisements to the public or employees regarding openings, promotions, transfers, training programs, or opportunities for overtime work. Employee benefit programs, written seniority or merit.	Three years. One year from date of personnel action to which the record relates, except 90 days for applications and other pre-employment records of applicants for temporary jobs. This period the plan is in effect plus one year.		Consolidated EEO poster.
Vocational Rehabilitation Act	Federal government contractors and subcontractors with a contract of $2500 or more.	Complete and accurate employment records for all handicapped applicants and employees. DOL suggests a notation in each person's application or file to indicate each vacancy, promotion, or training program for which s/he was considered including a statement of reason as to how that person was compared to others' qualifications as well as special accommodation considered. Description of these accommodations should be attached. Records regarding complaints or action taken under the Act.	One year. One year.	No filing required.	Consolidated EEO poster.

Statute	Employers Affected	Requirements	Period of Retention	When Required	Posting Required
Vietnam Era Veterans Readjustment Act	Federal government contractors and subcontractors with a contract of $10,000 or more.	Copies of reports to state employment service regarding number of individuals and veterans of the Vietnam era, both non-disabled and disabled, hired, and related documentation, such as personnel records, respective job openings, recruitment and placement. Records regarding complaints under the Act.	One year after final payment under contract. One year.		Consolidated EEO poster.
Fair Labor Standards Act	Employers engaged in interstate commerce.	Basic records containing employee information, payroll, individual contracts, or collective bargaining agreements, applicable certificates and notices of Wate-Hour Administrator, sales and purchase records. Supplementary basic records including employment and earning and records and wage rate tables. Also work time schedules, including order shipping and billing records. Records of additions to or deductions from wages paid. Documentation for basis of payment of any wage differential to employees of the opposite sex in the same establishment. Certificates of age. Written training agreements.	Three years. Two years. Until termination of employment. Duration of training program.		FLSA notice to employers. Consolidated EEO poster.
Davis Bacon Act	Employers on public Construction contracts exceeding $2000.	Pay minimum wages found by Labor Secretary to be prevailing in the area. Payroll records and classification of each laborer and mechanic, rate of pay, daily. Retain unexpired certificates of age for employed minors.	Three years from date of completion of contract. Period of employment.		Notice to employees of wage scale to be paid. No posting required.
Walsh-Healey Public Contracts Act	Employers holding federal contacts.	Records including name, address, sex, date of birth, and occupation. Also wage and hour records with contract number. Earnings records, wage rate tables and time schedules. Records & annual summary of illnesses and injuries.	Three years from date of last entry. Two years from date of last entry or last effective date. Three years after date of entry.		
Immigration Reform and Control Act of 1986	All employers regardless of size.	All employees must complete INS form I-9 and provide proof of eligibility to work in the U.S. within three days of hire.	Three years after date of hire or one year after employee termination, whichever is later. (Best to maintain records indefinitely.)	No filing required.	No posting required. Consolidated EEO poster.

Sample Compensation Plan

CHAMPION
SOFTWARE CORPORATION

Compensation Plan

I. Introduction

It is important for each employee of Champion Software Corporation (C.S.C.) to understand the company's compensation policies and procedures. The purpose of this document is to provide basic information about job evaluation, the salary structure and the administration of the Compensation Plan.

II. Compensation Objectives

C.S.C. wants each employee to be paid compensation that:

- Rewards good performance.
- Fairly reflects the duties and responsibilities of each position.
- Is competitive in the market place.
- Will attract, motivate and retain competent persons.
- Is internally equitable.
- Is cost effective for the company.

III. Job Description and Position Evaluation

Each employee, with his/her supervisor should complete a position information form or a job description, which will be used in the job evaluation process.

Also, each employee is urged to review his/her job description annually and to discuss it with the immediate supervisor. The Human Resources Department should be advised whenever there are significant changes in responsibilities of a position so that a job evaluation review may be completed.

In determining the relative worth of one position to another, many factors are considered, such as: Frequency and types of business decisions made.

- Frequency and types of analytical and creative output expected of the position.
- Independent actions and decisions that directly impact the sales and profitability of the company.
- Frequency and importance of relationships with customers, suppliers, shareholders, the general public, government agencies and other C.S.C. departments.
- Numbers and types of positions supervised directly and indirectly.
- The size arid type of budgetary responsibilities.
- Special Skills or knowledge required to perform a job.

- The minimum formal education required to perform a job in a satisfactory manner.

- The minimum experience required to perform a job in a satisfactory manner.

It is important to note that job evaluation is concerned with the content of a job and the evaluation into a salary grade — not with the performance of an individual in the job.

IV. Salary Ranges

Each job is assigned to a specific salary grade. Frequently, more than one job will be in a particular salary grade. Together, all salary grades comprise the company's salary structure. The salary range represents the "going rate" in the market place for trained, experienced persons.

Each salary grade will have a minimum, mid-point and maximum salary for all positions in the grade. The minimum salary is a fair rate for a person who just meets the basic qualifications of a job, with little or no experience. The mid-point of the salary range is considered an appropriate rate of pay for all experienced, fully qualified, competent employee performing all duties and responsibilities of the position in a completely satisfactory manner. The maximum of the salary range is the upper limit of potential dollar value of a position to C.S.C.

Each employee will be informed of his/her salary grade and the range of the grade.

V. Salary Surveys

To ensure that C.S.C. salary ranges are competitive with companies of comparable size in similar businesses, C.S.C. will participate in periodic salary surveys. The results of the surveys will be reviewed by the Human Resources Department and the officers of C.S.C. Salary ranges will be adjusted when necessary to remain competitive.

VI. Salary Administration

Job evaluation and salary structures deal with positions, their value to C.S.C., and their assignment to a salary grade. Salary administration involves managing and processing employee salaries. The policy of C.S.C. is to base each employee's salary primarily on work performance—the business results that an individual achieves which contribute to the growth and profitability of the company.

Annually, the chief executive officer of C.S.C. will approve a budget for merit salary increases, based on recommendations by the Human Resources Department. Within departments, the size of each employee's merit salary increase will be governed by:

- His/her performance on the job.

- Elapsed time since the last increase.

- The employee's current quartile in the salary range.

- The employee's recent salary history.

- The relationship of the employee salary to his/her peer group within the department.

VII. Performance Measurements

Performance Standards

For each major responsibility of a position, performance standards will be established by each employee in cooperation with his/her supervisor, which describe when a specific position responsibility is being done in a satisfactory manner.

Business Goals

At the start of each business year, incumbents of managerial and professional positions will also develop a few personal business goals, above the basic position responsibilities, which he/she commits to accomplish in a specified time period.

VIII. Performance Evaluation

At least annually the performance of each employee must be evaluated by the immediate supervisor and reviewed by the department head. Normally, this will be close to the anniversary date of the employee.

Each employee will be given a performance rating from one of the following:

O. Outstanding

Optimum performance in meeting every basis position responsibility and individual business goals.

A person in this category has comprehensive knowledge about his/her field and is highly experienced. This person achieves significantly more in quantity and quality than other employees. He or she may bring exceptional creativity to the job. This person exercises rare business judgment and the performance usually shows a broad understanding of more than his/her own work.

An individual in this category represents outstanding worth to Champion Software in his/her position. This person requires minimal direction.

E. Excellent

This employee frequently exceeds the basic position requirements on some of the most difficult and complex parts of the job. He/she will also achieve some individual business goals in a timely manner.

This person requires less supervision than a person the "G. Good" category. The individual frequently contributes a "little extra", anticipates problems and takes appropriate action.

G. Good

This employee is performing all basic position responsibilities in an acceptable manner. The performance is that expected of a qualified trained individual in the assigned position. Most work or projects are completed on schedule.

This person requires normal supervision and direction. However, the work of this individual probably requires more careful and frequent review than a person in a higher category.

M. Marginal

A person in this category is not performing some of the basic responsibilities of the position in a satisfactory manner, and also misses deadlines. This person may lack basic training and/or experience, which must be gained on the job.

Frequent and close supervision from the immediate supervisor is required and regular, careful reviews of the individual's work probably is necessary. With attention and application, the performance of a person in this category should rise to an acceptable level within a reasonable time frame.

A person in this category who does not improve to a "G. Good" level after a reasonable period should be assigned to another less demanding position or terminated by the company.

U. Unsatisfactory

A person in this category is failing to meet many basic position responsibilities and/or is particularly deficient in one or more of them. Frequently, this individual will need a disproportionate amount of guidance and direction from the supervisor.

Usually both the quality and quantity of the work are deficient and/or the person frequently misses deadlines.

A person in this category must be advised that his/her work is unsatisfactory and the reasons why. After counseling, a reasonable period should be established for prompt, significant improvement in job performance. If a satisfactory level is not reached after a probation period, the individual should be demoted or terminated.

Generally, in a business organization, not more than 10-15% of employees can truly be noticed as outstanding performers and only 20-25% are really excellent. Usually, a majority of individuals should be classified as "good performers" in their jobs.

IX. Salary Administration

Merit Increases

The job performance of an employee should be the primary consideration in making a salary increase decision. However, other factors, such as the total merit budget for a department and the employee's position in the salary range will also influence the size of the increase.

Usually, an employee's salary will be reviewed once a year on his/her anniversary date. Normally, retroactive increases will not be granted. Increases will become effective on either the 15th or 31st day of the month following final approval of the increase.

A Personnel Action form must be prepared by the immediate supervisor and approved by the department head. The Human Resources Department must review and approve each proposed increase to insure consistency and compliance with C.S.C. policies and procedures.

Promotional Increase Guidelines

A promotion results when an employee is given different and significantly larger job responsibilities that cause the position to be moved to a higher salary grade.

(Note: An increase in the volume of the same work performed by an individual is not a promotion). Depending on a variety of factors, a promotional increase may range up to 20% of the salary in the former position. Usually, the increase will become effective when the employee assumes the new responsibilities. However, sometimes an employee must spend an orientation or training period in the new position before he/she can perform the duties in an acceptable manner. In such cases, the promotional increase should be deferred until the orientation and training period are completed. Normally a promotional increase should be large enough so that the new salary is at least at the minimum of the new salary grade.

Merit Progression Guidelines

Some positions are members of the job families, (e.g. Account I, II, III and Programmer I, II, III). Based on pre-established criteria developed between the head of a department and the Human Resources Department (such as education, experience, job skills, job knowledge, tenure in the position and performance), the department head may advance an individual through the job family grade. An employee so advanced may be given a merit progression increase up to five percent.

Special Salary Adjustments

Usually, the salaries of new employees will be reviewed in less than one year:

- Between three and six months for non-exempt employees.
- Between six and nine months for exempt personnel

Merit increases may be granted depending on performance and other appropriate factors, e.g., completion of the orientation and training period.

Salary Decreases

It is not the policy of C.S.C. to decrease salaries except in extraordinary circumstances such as the demotion of an employee to a lower salary grade. However, even after a demotion, the salary will be decreased only if it exceeds the maximum of the new lower salary grade.

Recruiting Strategies

1. Mediums for Your Message

The number of ways to reach your target audience is enormous. They range from the conventional to the outrageous. But with the tightening of labor pools, organizations are turning to unusual ways to attract attention.

While image remains a consideration, even conservative firms like banks are finding that aggressive marketing strategies are the keys to recruitment. Here is a selection of proven mediums for reaching the people you want:

Airplane banners are an effective way to attract attention at large outdoor events and recreational areas like beaches. A short message with a phone number has yielded large numbers of applicants.

Billboards have been used extensively in the silicon valley for instance, to recruit technical professionals for computer firms. This technique works equally as well for other positions.

Bumper stickers with a recruiting slogan and a phone number appeal to people looking for work in an unassertive manner. Catchy phrases also attract those looking for a change of environment.

Busses, both school and public, have caught on as an effective form of advertising since people are spending more time in their cars. You might also integrate a recruitment promotion into existing ads on busses.

Career fairs can be used to fill current openings but more importantly for promoting your organization to various labor pools. Little giveaways in exchange for completing a short application yields a large number of potential applicants to contact in the future.

Cinema billboards and those around areas of entertainment get the attention of younger individuals contemplating a summer or part-time job. These advertisements should be lighthearted and convey the idea of having fun while working.

Direct mail has been used in situations where a large number of employees are needed. While rather involved, this technique reaches hundreds of potential applicants with relatively little expense. Mailing lists can be obtained from specific organizations from whom you would like to recruit and/or from list brokers who can provide names based on demographics, zip codes and a host of other variables.

You might also include fliers about available job opportunities in your other direct mail you send. Potential customers can be potential employees.

Door hangers are effective in situations where the geography of potential applicants is limited. This includes retail recruiting around apartment complexes, colleges and military bases.

Envelope stuffers can be inserted into your customers' mail like their bills, newsletters, product information and stockholder reports. These applicants may be some of your best since they already support your products.

Internet postings on the World Wide Web can reach millions of people at once and can be updated quickly and inexpensively. The key is to develop a description that is attention getting and focused on the values of your target audience. You may also be able to gather resumes by searching the Web under keywords associated with your industry.

Job fairs are an excellent way to showcase opportunities within your operation. They are generally aimed at specific groups such as engineers, technicians and those in demand. In addition to the exposure to applicants, you can also observe other companies' tactics for recruiting.

Kiosks offer the opportunity to advertise openings in high traffic areas. You may obtain space on kiosks in shopping malls, centers of entertainment, college campuses and other public areas. In addition, you might build or purchase mobile kiosks to place in areas your targeted groups frequent. Be careful however to obtain necessary permission before doing so.

Leaflet distribution can be another way to attract the attention of those seeking part-time or supplementary income. Quick-reading, aggressively written fliers with simple contact instructions work the best. Once again, obtain the appropriate permission before distributing.

Magnetic signs work well in a variety of situations such as the sides of company vans and trailers or on steel warehouses. These messages should be exciting and to the point with easy contact instructions.

Open houses play to the public's curiosity about your organization. You can take advantage of this by opening your doors and conducting interesting tours. A recruiting booth can be set up at the end to encourage applications.

Point of sale in retail situations, quick, informative fliers will catch the eye of potential applicants. If they like your store maybe they would like to work for you, or know someone who does.

Posters with tear-off coupons make applying convenient for those who might hesitate about taking the trouble to call or visit your employment office. Returned coupons can be followed with a phone call and application.

Presentations to local groups can serve several purposes including recruiting. All company representatives should address job opportunities as part of every presentation. You don't know who might be listening.

Radio can be an excellent medium for attracting applicants. The commercials should be tailored to the listening audience. Phrases such as "call today" or "stop by right now!" really work.

Telemarketing, like direct mail, is an involved process, but it is also extremely effective if properly conducted. Research your target markets. Develop the "pitch," and train those calling potential employees on how to represent the company. For professional level positions, you might even involve managers in a phone campaign. Most applicants find "being recruited" an attractive proposition.

Television, though expensive in most cities, can be an effective means for attracting applicants. Daytime and late night are the best times to reach those out of work. The ads should be exciting and convenience-oriented, such as, "call our office right now at 123-4567 and join our team!"

Trade shows, while not geared specifically for recruiting, offer you the opportunity to make contact with a large number of people within your industry. Blatant recruiting may be discouraged, but you should always be prepared to discuss opportunities.

Transit advertising is perfect for reaching those commuters who are working in your vicinity. Travel to and from work tends to be a considerable issue. Addressing this in your advertising will encourage them to think about joining your organization. Transit advertising also demonstrates to those out of work that they can reach your business without a car.

2. Developing Innovative Strategies

Now that you are aware of the variety of mediums available, the next step is to decide how to make best use of them. This section covers 50 strategies that have been used by companies for recruiting the right people. As you might imagine, each theme has many variations. Adapt them to your benefit.

Overall strategies

These strategies take a commitment on the part of the entire organization and are generally long-term projects. The results however, can be phenomenal if they are executed with enthusiasm and follow-through.

Develop better relations with local schools. The overall goals for doing this are two-fold: 1) to improve applicants' skills and, 2) attract attention to your company. Meet with the local principal or superintendent and discuss ways you can help such as organizing tutoring programs, sponsoring contests and other events. Arrange presentations by "role model" employees or employees who attended that school. Co-sponsor a "business week" or a booster club for academic achievement. You might also work through business groups that have on-going programs.

Research and access employee pools from downsizing organizations. Even in a strong economy, there are always companies laying off employees. When these be come apparent in your area, approach their management about holding a "job opportunity meeting" with those being released.

Stay up to date on personnel in other organizations who may be available. Massage the network of professionals and executives on a regular basis. Attending association meetings and civic functions will keep you abreast of who's doing what, where.

Initiate a retiree job bank. Every year, companies lose good employees to retirement. Yet studies indicate that most of these individuals would still like to contribute. Organize a program to incorporate your retirees into part-time, temporary roles. They can also serve in consulting and training positions. Take advantage of this tremendous source of experienced and loyal labor.

Invite retirees from other companies to "un-retire." A number of companies have developed programs to recruit retirees from other local companies to work for them. Not only have they found enthusiastic support for this, they have also been able to locate individuals already skilled in the areas needed.

Conduct programs that shepherd high school students through college and into your company. A number of organizations have implemented programs that assist minorities and the underprivileged through high school programs and college. They also provide summer employment and internships. In return, it is hoped that these individuals will join the company on a full-time basis after graduation.

Initiate a "telecommuting" program. A number of insurance companies have instituted arrangements where the employee works at home four days per week and commutes to the office on the fifth day. The company provides the necessary equipment and materials, such as computer, telephone modem and desk, to allow the employee to function without leaving the home. This has opened up new possibilities for those who are home-bound, parents with small children and individuals who have trouble with transportation. In addition, it allows the company to recruit in a larger geographic area since commuting is not an issue.

Expand your use of temporaries and part-timers. More and more operations are adapting their personnel needs to fill positions with individuals who work on a non-full-time basis. In addition to saving money on benefits, these people are more flexible and project oriented. While temporaries are generally more expensive, this is offset by the fact that you are not committed to them on a long-term basis.

Offer job sharing opportunities. This is not a new concept, but one that has been accepted in relatively few companies. While there are sometimes difficulties in continuity and supervision, your organization's willingness to adapt to this practice can open up a large pool of individuals interested in working only part-time. These groups include highly trained parents bringing up small children and semi-retired professionals with no interest in returning to full-time.

Train supervisors to accept and cope with non-traditional applicants and their issues. As the labor force grows more diverse, supervisors will be faced with a variety of situations and issues. These include child and elder care responsibilities, language differences, transportation problems and cultural conflicts. Their coping with and making the most of these events will result in better employee relations, higher productivity and lower turnover. Do not assume supervisors will automatically adapt to these challenges. Training in cultural and social issues is essential.

Initiate an internship program. Thousands of organizations across the United States conduct internship programs in conjunction with local colleges. Internships give students the opportunity to apply those skills they have learned. The advantages for the organization are manifold including the training and development of a high performing employee after graduation. Remember however, that these individuals should not be hired to perform simple clerical duties. If they do not have the opportunity to practice their interests, they will probably sour on the organization.

Re-hire those who have left. While this has been frowned upon in the past, re-hiring former employees can save the company significant time and money. This is especially true for those with in-demand skills. Obviously, care should be taken to review the circumstances under which they left.

Position the company as an organization that is "committed to the importance of family." As society evolves, family issues appear to be taking on additional importance in the minds of employees. The days of working 80 hour weeks seem to be subsiding. Positioning your company's image as one who is concerned about the balance between work and family will attract the large group of workers who are mindful of this situation.

Incentives

These features can be used as "come-ons" to attract certain pools of applicants. The use of them in a recruiting campaign should be tailored to the audience.

While some of these may be used directly in the campaign to attract applicants, others can be used more indirectly to improve employee relations and encourage those already working for the organization to recommend others:

Shared housing for employees can be especially helpful in tight housing markets or recreational locales. Ski resorts for example, go so far as to build dormitories on their property to house winter workers.

Subsidized housing for employees relieves the strain of having to locate affordable accommodations in an expensive locale. In some cases, a housing allowance is provided. In others, the company steps in to negotiate better deals with landlords.

Commuter rail and bus passes are of tremendous assistance to those in areas such as New York and San Francisco where the daily commute can cost more than five dollars. You might be able to purchase these passes at a discount and use them in a variety of ways to attract applicants.

Company operated van services transport employees from outside the local area to their site. An indirect effect of this is that it forces employees to be on time.

Company operated escort services transport employees to and from company sites for purposes of security. For plants located in undesirable areas, this may the best way to overcome applicant hesitation.

Employee parking lots are a great attraction in large cities or other areas where parking is a problem. In some cases, companies provide shuttles to outlying lots.

Full-time benefits for part-time employees is a very attractive come-on especially for those in single parent situations. Although this can be an expensive proposition, you must weigh this against the opportunity to recruit good people.

Relocation programs for the most part have been confined to professional and executive level hiring. In certain cases however, a superior candidate may be lured with a small stipend to subsidize actual moving expenses.

Sign-on bonuses have been traditionally used to entice executives. But small bonuses, especially in cash, can be very attractive. One company for instance, went so far as to give out $100 bills to employees on their first day of work. (The taxes for this were accounted for in the first paycheck.)

Sponsored entertainment events, especially for families, can have a very positive impact on how employees perceive the company. Getting as many employees involved as possible also increases morale.

Employee appreciation programs demonstrate your interest in the staff. Ideas such as plaques, flowers, dinners and "employee of the month" parking spaces will boost employee interest. This interest can be translated into referrals of applicants.

Meetings with employee groups to air concerns is an excellent means for staying in touch with the company environment and provides the opportunity to encourage recruitment. It is paramount however, that follow through takes place on commitments. Without this, all credibility is lost.

Employee referral programs can generate constant stream of qualified applicants since they are being referred by those who work in your organization. Adding a cash incentive will create even more enthusiasm.

Creative techniques

The following strategies have been used successfully to recruit employees. While you may find some inappropriate for your organization, most can be adapted to work for you:

Contests featuring substantial cash awards can be implemented to reward employees who actively recruit applicants. This type of program can also be tied to an incentive where the longer the hired recruit stays with the company, the more money the referring employee gets.

Eligibility for drawings to win cash prizes is an alternative to the above and might also be designed to include newly hired applicants.

Successful job applicants become eligible for drawing for an automobile is still another alternative and might also be designed as an incentive for employees.

Brochures promoting job opportunities can be distributed to employees to use when they meet potential applicants. You might also distribute a little "cheat sheet" of benefits to bring up.

Business card size applications that employees can give to interested individuals is an attention getting gimmick. While every applicant will have to complete a full application when they visit the organization, these smaller versions can be used as a pre-screening device.

Personalized recruitment advertisements have worked extremely well in hiring for clerical and support staff. They are placed in the classifieds but take a different approach.

Layered information in advertising attracts the attention of applicants through the use of curiosity. The Bank of Boston for instance used the words "temporary sanity" at the top of their recruiting advertisements for temporaries.

Print and broadcast ads in languages associated with the community demonstrate your organization's interest in working with those around it. A large number of referrals may also result from this since these communities tend to be close-knit.

Posters aimed at foreign students printed in their language displayed on college campuses attract the attention of these individuals. Some American electronics firms operating in Japan for instance, recruit Japanese students to work in their home country when they graduate.

Visiting executives at colleges and high schools, while not a direct recruiting tactic, can produce tremendous goodwill and notoriety. These individuals can teach classes, consult with faculty, sponsor events and a host of other ideas.

Promotions with media to attract applicants such as contests, charity events and fun runs can generate awareness of the company and its participation in the community. Not only can public relations benefit but the organization is receiving the indirect endorsement of the station or publication.

Celebrity hosted events attract attention and promote good-will in the community. These individuals can be used in programs such as the opening of a new plant, debut of a product or the beginning of a recruiting campaign. Once they have attracted the crowd, it is up to you to sign up the applicants.

Give personal attention to those who leave the company by keeping in touch with cards and letters. Check up on how they are doing. Many return.

On-site interviews in malls, job service agencies, and other public places make the application process convenient for those who might be interested. Some large companies with high turnover have established permanent store front in malls to enhance recruiting of students and older individuals who frequent these locations.

A telephone job line with the latest opportunities is a convenient way for those interested in work to discover what positions are available. In a busy company, getting through the receptionist is sometimes difficult. Having a dedicated line for applicants will provide an information source while not disrupting other company business.

Toll-free numbers simply encourage applicants to apply at no cost to them. This holds especially true for graduating college students who are applying out of state.

Return postage guaranteed simply makes it easier for applicants to reply, especially those who are economically disadvantaged.

Mobile recruiting vans take the recruiting effort to the applicants. These can be parked at shopping malls, sporting events, and other large gatherings. Be sure however to obey local parking ordinances and to obtain the necessary permissions.

Advertising to your customers through direct mail and envelope stuffers can be a great way to obtain referrals. If they like your product, they'll refer people or perhaps apply themselves.

Local teachers' unions and school districts can be tremendous sources of labor during the summer. Approach local schools early in the spring to ask about making presentations at meetings and sending invitations to their faculty.

Revive the dead resume file. While some of these applications may be several months old, there is no guarantee that these individuals have found work. A ten second phone call will establish this.

Ask applicants being interviewed for the names of 2 or 3 other people who might be interested in positions. These off-chance referrals can provide some excellent candidates.

Asking for referrals of other people on applications is a variation of the above. Since some people do not make it into the interview process, asking a question like this on the application garners all referrals possible.

Advertise that a training session will begin in the next week and see who shows up. Some people do not apply for jobs because they think they don't have the training. If you eliminate that obstacle, you may find they are very interested in your organization. After they have contacted you about the training session, they can then be screened for suitability.

Develop a slogan specific to recruiting. The Los Angeles Police Department uses "Color me blue." and "Be somebody. Be a cop," in its recruiting campaigns. Quick and memorable sayings come to an applicant's mind and provide a value with which they can identify.

Hot air balloons are great attention getters and can be used in a variety of ways. The only caution here is to research and observe the laws and ordinances associated with these vehicles. As you can see, when it comes to recruiting employees, the sky has become the limit! The same rules and techniques used to market your product can be adapted to hiring people.

Index